W9-BUH-940

The Role of Policymakers in Business Cycle Fluctuations

The book's central theme is that a policymaker's role is to enhance the public's ability to coordinate its price information, price expectations, and economic activities. The role is fulfilled when policymakers maintain inflation stability. Inflation persists less when an implicit or explicit inflation target is met. Granato and Wong argue that inflation persistence is reduced when the public substitutes the prespecified inflation target for past inflation. A byproduct of this coordination process is greater economic stability. In particular, inflation stability contributes to greater economic output stability, including the potential for the simultaneous reduction of both inflation and output variability – inflation-output costabilization (IOCS). Granato and Wong use historical, formal, and applied statistical analysis of business cycle performance in the United States for the 1960–2000 period. They find, for example, that during periods when policymakers emphasize inflation stability, inflation uncertainty and persistence were reduced.

JIM GRANATO is Adjunct Associate Professor in the Department of Government at the University of Texas at Austin. Prior to his current position, he was Visiting Scientist and Political Science Program Director in the Political Science Program of the National Science Foundation (NSF). He is the author or co-author of numerous publications in academic journals such as *American Journal of Political Science, Economics and Politics, Journal of Theoretical Politics, Political Analysis, Political Research Quarterly, Public Choice,* and the *Southern Economic Journal.*

M. C. SUNNY WONG is Assistant Professor of Economics at the University of Southern Mississippi. His primary research has focused on adaptive learning dynamics in monetary policy, and he is also interested in the areas of foreign direct investment (FDI) and economic growth. Professor Wong has published research articles in such journals as the *Journal of Macroeconomics, Political Research Quarterly,* and the *Southern Economic Journal.*

The Role
of Policymakers
in Business Cycle
Fluctuations

—— ‡ ——

Jim Granato

University of Texas at Austin

M. C. Sunny Wong

University of Southern Mississippi

CAMBRIDGE
UNIVERSITY PRESS

CAMBRIDGE UNIVERSITY PRESS
Cambridge, New York, Melbourne, Madrid, Cape Town, Singapore, São Paulo

Cambridge University Press
40 West 20th Street, New York, NY 10011-4211, USA

www.cambridge.org
Information on this title: www.cambridge.org/9780521860161

First published 2006

Printed in the United States of America

A catalog record for this publication is available from the British Library.

Library of Congress Cataloging in Publication Data

Granato, Jim, 1960–
The role of policymakers in business cycle fluctuations / Jim Granato,
M. C. Sunny Wong.
p. cm.
Includes bibliographical references and index.
ISBN-13: 978-0-521-86016-1 (hardback)
ISBN-10: 0-521-86016-4 (hardback)
1. Economic policy. 2. Business cycles. 3. Inflation (Finance)
I. Wong, M. C. Sunny, 1976– . II. Title.
HD87.5.G73 2006
338.5′42 – dc22 2005037077

ISBN-13 978-0-521-86016-1 hardback
ISBN-10 0-521-86016-4 hardback

For our parents,
Dolores Mistro Granato, James Lawrence Granato,
Sing Luen Tam, Chi Kong Wong
And our wives,
Helen Au Yeung, Mary Bange

Contents

Contents

Contents

Contents

Contents

Figures

Figures

Figures

Tables

Preface

If business cycles were simply efficient responses of quantities and prices to unpredictable shifts in technology and preferences, there would be no need for distinct stabilization or demand management policies. . . . If, on the other hand, rigidities of some kind prevent the economy from reacting efficiently to nominal or real shocks, or both, there is a need to design suitable policies and to assess their performance. In my opinion, this is the case: I think the stability of monetary aggregates and nominal spending in the postwar United States is a major reason for the stability of aggregate production and consumption during these years, relative to the experience of the interwar period and the contemporary experience of other economies.

Robert E. Lucas Jr. (2003: 11)

The theory of economic policy occupies a central place in academia and government. This book addresses concerns in both communities. For academics, this book examines the ongoing scientific endeavor to determine the most accurate representation of the business cycle and what the optimal role for policymakers is in stabilizing it.[1] Scientific controversies center on such issues as the relation between inflation and real outcomes and how these disagreements influence the supposed effectiveness of policy.[2] In more technical language, a particular scientific controversy of interest to us is the evolution in thinking about the slope of the Phillips curve and how this has influenced policy and outcomes (see Akerlof et al. 2000).

[1] There are numerous definitions of the business cycle. The U.S. Congressional Budget Office (CBO) uses but also credits the National Bureau of Economic Research (NBER) with the following definition (see http://www.cbo.gov/showdoc.cfm?index= 3280&sequence=0):

Fluctuations in overall business activity accompanied by swings in the unemployment rate, interest rates, and corporate profits. Over a business cycle, real activity rises to a peak (its highest level during the cycle), then falls until it reaches a trough (its lowest level following the peak), whereupon it starts to rise again, defining a new cycle. Business cycles are irregular, varying in frequency, magnitude, and duration (NBER).

Classic work in the study of business cycles can be found in Burns and Mitchell (1946) and Mitchell (1913, 1951). More technical and modern treatments of business cycles can be found in Diebold and Rudebusch (1999), Sargent (1987), and Zarnowitz (1996).

[2] Because inflation is primarily a monetary phenomenon, we focus on monetary policy.

On the other hand, policymakers – a term that includes policy advisors to the executive administration and members of the monetary authority (who can be either research scientists or decision makers, or both) – are focused on, for example, taking the right policy action at the right time. Yet, there is no doubt that policymaker discretion has been influenced by changing scientific conceptions of the Phillips curve. Policy goals or targets, long a concern of policymakers, receive more or less weight based not only on current economic conditions but also on what science says is the optimal course of action. To be more specific, policy trade-offs between inflation (inflation variability) and real economic factors (and their variability) are dictated in part by the academic consensus on the slope of the Phillips curve. This scientific debate includes whether and when these trade-offs even exist. An issue for policymakers, then, is the degree to which they rely on such research as opposed to just using common sense.[3]

Although the academic and policymaking communities have different ways of looking at the world, we contend that it would be a mistake to treat these two groups separately. Academics analyze the effects of actual policy, whereas

[3] See Blinder (1998) and Carpenter (2004).

policymakers use the analysis of scholars when implementing policy. In a real sense, this book is an argument for blurring the distinction between academics and policymakers. The integration of practical policy concerns – with a thorough social scientific examination of the process of how policy influences business cycle outcomes – is one aim of this book.

Furthermore, in matters of policy, academics and policymakers each need the expertise of the other to avoid policy errors. In the United States, during the 1930s, policymakers failed to engage in stimulative monetary policy when economic theory dictated that course of action (Friedman and Schwartz 1963; Meltzer 2003). The Great Depression was the result. At the other extreme, the stagflation of the 1970s occurred because the academic consensus supported the idea of a structural Phillips curve that policymakers could control, but policymaker "experience" suggested otherwise (see also Lucas 1980; Sargent 1999).[4]

---

[4] Examples of the interplay between scientific research and policymaker experience are found in Meyer (2004). For example, on the relation among productivity, wages, and inflation he states, "Economic theory tells us that a leap in productivity will raise wages in the long run. But experience tells us that wages are not initially much affected. As a result, in the short term, an increase in productivity

The issue of when to take the right course of action, then, is not just a matter of luck. The fusion of scientific research with practical day-to-day policy activity cannot totally eliminate harmful policy choices, given the uncertainties of certain scientific relations and the pressure of making real-time decisions, but greater collaboration cannot hurt either.[5] Alan Greenspan (2004) suggests that peaceful coexistence is possible in the conduct of policy:

> In designing strategies to meet our policy objectives, we have drawn on the work of analysts. . . . A critical result has been the identification of a relatively small set of key relationships that, taken together, provide a useful approximation of the economy's dynamics. . . . However, . . . our knowledge about many of the important linkages is far from complete and, in all likelihood, will always remain so. . . . For such judgment, policymakers have needed to reach beyond models to broader – though less mathematically precise – hypotheses about how the world works. (pp. 5, 7)

Against this background, we consider the role of policymakers in business cycle fluctuations. We argue that the

tends to lower the cost per unit of output. This, in turn, will generally push prices down" (p. 126).

[5] Söderström and Vredin (2000) refer to this fusion as a *complete reorientation of monetary policy* where "politicians and central bankers learned from experience (and from economic theory)" (p. 8).

overriding role of policymakers is to harness both scientific and practical acumen to assist in coordinating economic (that is, price) information so that the marketplace functions efficiently. The specific way to fulfill this role is to ensure inflation stability. Although inflation stability can coincide with other macroeconomic goals, we view inflation *in*stability as a preventable cause of economic affliction. Inflation stability does not guarantee economic prosperity, but its absence presages harmful economic consequences. We also argue that achieving inflation stability can coincide with further stability in aggregate output.

This book is a mix of narrative, formal modeling, and econometrics. It is geared toward the academic and policy audience. The people most comfortable with this material will be graduate students, fellow academics, professionals, and policymakers with a working knowledge of the issues and the technical approach. We also think that there is sufficient nontechnical material to enable upper-level undergraduates to grasp the main arguments. This book would be useful for courses in macropolitical economy, macroeconomic policy, and monetary policy; courses that examine learning dynamics; and methodological courses that need examples that merge formal and empirical analysis.

Preface

Many individuals read either all or portions of this project and made valuable comments and criticisms. We thank Bill Bernhard, Norman Bradburn, Michelle Costanzo, John Freeman, Richard Lempert, Jack Medick, and Joan Sieber. We also have benefited enormously from the collaboration(s) with Mark Jones, Bill Keech, Melody Lo, and Miao Wang. We also thank James Bullard for the use of his data.

A portion of this book is based on Wong's dissertation, which was written while he was at the University of Oregon. The comments and criticisms of Shankha Chakraborty, George Evans, Steven Haynes, and John Orbell are gratefully acknowledged.

This material is also based, in part, on work supported by (while Granato served at) the National Science Foundation. Frank Scioli's invaluable feedback and support made working at the National Science Foundation an unforgettably positive experience. We also want to thank Peggy Rote and Sandra Sizer for their expert editorial work. A final thank you to Simina Calin, Brianne Millett, Steven Mosier, Marielle Poss, and, especially, Scott Parris at Cambridge University Press for their comments and assistance through the entire review and publication process.

Preface

Any opinions, findings, and conclusions or recommendations expressed in this material are those of the author(s) and do not necessarily reflect the views of the National Science Foundation.

— ‡ **PART I** ‡ —

The Interaction of Policy and Outcomes

CHAPTER ONE

Coordinating Price Information

The fact that the public must learn about underlying economic relationships changes the nature of the optimal monetary policy.... [A]
central bank should work actively to "anchor" inflation expectations
within a narrow range.... [E]fficient policy in this world requires
that policymakers pay attention to information (for example, from
surveys) about the public's expectations of inflation and other variables; if these appear not to be converging toward the desired levels,
then a policy response may be warranted.

Ben S. Bernanke (2004: 5–6)

T he central theme of this book is that a macroeconomic
policymaker's role is to conduct policy in such a way as
to enhance the public's ability to coordinate its information,
expectations, and economic activities. Our view is that policy
actions that facilitate the public's coordination capability are
essential for ensuring a stable and predictable framework for

the rules that govern social and economic interaction. When policymakers encourage coordination, one of the primary consequences is efficient macroeconomic outcomes, the full employment of resources with price stability.[1]

There are several ideas, some prescriptive, some purely academic, that provide a foundation for this theme. First is the necessity for coordination. We use the term *coordination* to define the actions a person or persons take to interpret and order streams of information (primarily political and economic) and to use that information in making their economic plans.

---

[1] We define the *full employment of resources* as a situation in which output equals its natural rate. The term *natural rate* has been used in reference to unemployment (Friedman 1968). The natural rate of unemployment level is the long-term equilibrium unemployment level. Inflation is constant at this level of unemployment. In this book we also refer to the "natural (potential) rate" of output.

Price or inflation stability can be defined as the achievement of a prespecified inflation target (see Goodhart and Viñals 1994) or when citizens no longer account for actual or prospective inflation in their decision making (Volcker and Gyothen 1992). Svensson (1999) has offered a more technical distinction between price *level* stability and price stability (low and stable inflation). Price level stability implies stationarity around a deterministic trend, whereas price stability implies a nonstationary price level (such as base drift – the presence of a unit root). Because our focus is on low and stable inflation (assumed when using inflation targets), we use the term *inflation stability* in the text.

A second idea is that coordination involves strategic inter-action between policymakers and the public. This interaction can be conflictual. However, the emphasis in this book is on the policymaker and public interactions that include alternative factors, such as confidence, credibility, expectations, and learning, and how these interactions influence macroeconomic outcomes (Cooper and John 1988; Cooper 1999).

The third idea is that there are significant obstacles to public coordination, such as information asymmetries (Akerlof 1970) and the slow diffusion of information (Mankiw and Reis 2002). In the face of such obstacles, our task is to examine how, in a decentralized market setting, firms, households, and labor coordinate specific knowledge of the information in their immediate circumstances with their imperfect knowledge of their more general surroundings (Hayek 1945; Barro and Grossman 1976; Sowell 1980).

The fourth idea is that policymaker and public coordination is done under the auspices of the price system. In decentralized market economies, the price system can provide the necessary and relevant information to enable firms, households, and labor to devise plans that accurately reflect the signals of economic activity. A significant attribute of the price system is that it enables individuals to economize on the necessary and relevant information required to take the right action on economic matters (Groshen and Schweitzer 1996; Blinder 1998: 71–3).

In principle, the information provided by prices should help prevent coordination difficulties. Of course, during a period of inflation, prices lose their effectiveness in conveying information. Price inflation creates noise in the price system (see Friedman 1963). The usual signal that reduces the coordination problem is now blurred. Planning now lacks the accurate expectations it had under inflation stability. The ability to learn the appropriate signal from prices is also delayed (Friedman 1977).

To amplify this issue further, we think that price system distortions, caused by inflation instability, are more than an abstract academic argument. The social and economic costs of inflation instability are significant. Consider that the relation between inflation and output can be separated into both short- and long-term effects. In the short term, inflation can have a positive effect on output. For example, firms have limited information, and thus they make errors about the future prices they expect to receive (relative prices). These errors affect their production decisions. In particular, firms confuse an increase in the general price level (inflation) with an increase in the prices for their own goods (Lucas 1973).

The confusion between inflation and relative prices leads firms to increase their output above normal. Employment also increases during such periods.

However, this confusion is short-lived. With the passage of time, firms eventually correct their pricing errors and realize that the expected jump in prices was caused by inflation and not by an increase in demand for their own good(s). After having risen for "artificial" reasons, both output and employment now fall.

Along with the short-term volatility, inflation also can have adverse long-term consequences on growth (Fischer 1993, 1996; Andersen and Gruen 1995; Hess and Morris 1996; Judson and Orphanides 1996; Sarel 1996; Barro 1997; Bulman and Simon 2003). The public (firms, households, and labor) is encouraged to turn its attention away from wealth-producing ventures. As inflation rises, more resources are diverted to hedging and to speculation. Interaction with tax rules produces additional difficulties for firms as they manage their balance sheets (Abel 1997; Feldstein 1997). Consequently, capital inputs are reduced, and long-term planning becomes increasingly difficult because of the uncertainty of the real value of the expected future payments. The end result is that inflation reduces the scope and scale of activities that facilitate economic growth.

We also believe there is a relation between inflation stability and the duration of economic expansions. If we examine the business cycle performance of the United States since 1960, we find an almost continuously sustained expansion in the 1980s and 1990s and a similarly lengthy expansion in the 1960s. Furthermore, consider U.S. business cycle performance since 1982 in comparison to all peacetime expansions recorded since 1854. The average duration for peacetime business expansions since 1854 is 30.5 months. In contrast, the average duration of the two peacetime expansions between 1982 and 2002 was 106 months.[2] Inflation stability also accompanied the two recent long-lasting expansions.[3]

The fifth idea is prescriptive and concerns the role of policymakers in the environment sketched in this introduction.[4]

---

[2] See http://www.nber.org/cycles.html.

[3] Since 1854, the three longest economic expansions, peacetime or otherwise, coincided with inflation stability.

[4] Real business cycle (RBC) theory (see Kydland and Prescott 1982 and Long and Plosser 1983) provides an alternative perspective on short-term economic fluctuations. A central RBC argument is that nonmonetary factors, such as technological shocks, changes in government expenditures, and variations of tax rates, are the real disturbances behind business cycles. Further, RBC models typically assume that markets always clear and that real variables are independent of nominal variables. This approach leaves little or no role for countercyclical policy. Because we argue that coordinating effects of policy are important, we note only that the

Pervasive uncertainty about policy contributes to these adverse short- and long-term economic outcomes. In the face of this economic uncertainty, a policymaker's role is clear and imperative. We argue that policymakers should act to ensure that the price system works and that the coordinating function of prices is maintained. There is only one way to do this: policymakers must take policy actions that ensure inflation stability.[5] In achieving inflation stability, policymakers provide a clear "inflation target,"[6] and this gives notice to

RBC approach has made important contributions, but the lack of emphasis on countercyclical policy requires that we rely on an alternative modeling and theoretical approach. For an overview and critique of the RBC approach see Hansen and Heckman (1996), Kydland and Prescott (1996), Sheffrin (1989), and Sims (1996).

[5] We recognize the potential importance of policymaker rhetoric and public statements (see Kohn and Sack 2003 and Kuttner and Posen 1999). However, our specific focus is on policymaker actions.

[6] Bernanke et al. (1999) define inflation targeting as "a framework for monetary policy characterized by the public announcement of official quantitative targets (or target ranges) for the inflation rate over one or more time horizons, and by explicit acknowledgement that low, stable inflation is monetary policy's primary long-run goal" (p. 4).

Note the use of the word *framework,* a term used by Friedman (1948). The term implies that policymakers will commit in advance to general objectives, but with flexibility in action on how to counteract specific contingencies (i.e., events) that may deviate from the objectives (Bernanke et al. 1999: 6).

the public that will steer and then anchor its expectations[7] (Leiderman and Svensson 1995; Bruno and Easterly 1998; Bernanke et al. 1999).

In general, what we argue for is a policymaker role that is similar in spirit to that advocated by Friedman (1948) and Lucas (1980). Policymaker discretion is limited to a specific set of variables and relations that Lucas notes are "well-understood and empirically substantiated propositions of monetary economics" and that are known to assist "in providing a stable, predictable environment for the private sector of the economy" (p. 210).

As a consequence, the traditional stabilization policymaker role, in which a policymaker manages aggregate demand, usually to stimulate output and employment (Keynes

In related work, Leiderman and Svensson (1995) characterize an inflation target regime, in part, as "an explicit quantitative inflation target (specifying the index, the target level, the tolerance interval, the time frame, and possibly situations under which the inflation target will be modified or disregarded). Sometimes the inflation target has been announced jointly by the monetary and fiscal authorities, sometimes by the monetary authority alone" (p. 1). Leiderman and Svensson also note that a secondary characteristic of inflation targeting is the absence of an intermediate target for both monetary aggregates and exchange rates.

[7] See Goodfriend (1993) on the "inflation scare" – autonomous upward revisions in inflation expectations (reflected in increases in long-term interest rates) – problem.

1936), is now refined. Our view is that this traditional emphasis has led to policy errors by overstimulating the economy and by adding unnecessary noise in the signals that prices provide and that they are expected to provide. The point is not to ignore aggregate demand (output and employment) or deflationary concerns,[8] but instead to make inflation stability an implicit or explicit target (goal) for policy actions.

1.1 Features of the Book

There are several distinctive features of this study. One is the analytical and technical approach. We merge formal analysis directly with empirical tests and actual data. In the same spirit as Friedman (1957) and Lucas (1973), we

---

[8] An IMF report (2003) noted that "there have been few sustained deflationary episodes in the post–Second World War period in the major economies"(p. 15).

   We do not discount the possibility of a deflation. However, much of the harmful effects of a deflation occur when it is unanticipated (Fisher 1933). We contend that unanticipated deflation (or inflation) is extremely unlikely when a policymaker consistently achieves an inflation target (implicit or explicit) and thereby steers public expectations and plans. For an alternative view that emphasizes price rigidities in the adjustment process, see Akerlof et al. (1996).

show that specific empirical coefficients will fluctuate based on various changes in variables (parameters) in our formal model.

Whereas Friedman (1957) and Lucas (1973) took advantage of "error in variables" regression and combined it with permanent-temporary (Friedman) or general-relative confusion (Lucas), we use regression analysis to show that policymaker actions affect the persistence of a variable of interest and its attendant volatility.[9]

Another feature is that we incorporate an up-to-date treatment of agent expectations. We rely on an adaptive learning framework that includes (rational) expectations[10] and learning (bounded rationality), as well as the stability conditions that require the use of both (see Bray 1982; Sargent 1999; Evans and Honkapohja 2001; Evans and Guesnerie 2003; and Orphanides and Williams 2003a).[11]

[9] The linking of formal and empirical analysis is part of the Empirical Implications of Theoretical Models (EITM) initiative supported at the National Science Foundation. For more information see http://www.nsf.gov/sbe/ses/polisci/reports/eitmreport.jsp and http://www.nsf.gov/pubs/2003/nsf03552/nsf03552.pdf.
[10] Following Muth (1961), we define rational expectations as a condition and technique in which expectations within a model are the same as a model's own predictions.
[11] Bernanke (2004: 3) argues further that policymakers must consider the expectations of the public because "when the public does not

This framework results in agents "incorporating forecasting functions like those in rational expectations models but with coefficients that adapt to fit recent data" (Sargent and Söderström 2000: 16). The importance of this second feature is emphasized by Ben Bernanke (2004):

> In general, the problem is that the public's learning process *itself* affects the behavior of the economy – for example, as when expectational errors by bond traders affect interest rates and thus a wide range of economic decisions. The feedback effect of learning on the economy, this literature has shown, can in principle lead to unstable or indeterminate outcomes. More generally, the dynamic behavior of an economy with asymmetric information and learning may be radically different from the behavior of the same economy in the optimal rational expectations equilibrium. (p. 3)

A third feature is our view of policy as an alternative to the standard "time consistency" argument of Kydland and Prescott (1977) and Barro and Gordon (1983a, b).[12] We

---

know but instead must estimate the central bank's reaction function and other economic relationships using observed data, we have no guarantee that the economy will converge – even in infinite time – to the optimal rational expectations equilibrium."

[12] As it pertains to monetary policy, the theory of time (in)consistency suggests that it is not possible for policymakers to make a binding commitment to prevent inflation surprises (see Kydland and Prescott 1977).

argue that policymakers try to conduct countercyclical policy that is not intended to "fool" anyone. Instead, we assume policymakers behave in ways that mimic dynamic programming in which they "project an entire path of future monetary policy actions, with associated paths of key economic variables. ... [I]f things evolved as expected, it would keep following its projected path" (Blinder 1998: 16).

Although we acknowledge that the time consistency literature has led to important theoretical breakthroughs, particularly on "commitment problems" (see Cooper 1999: 141), we argue that this is not how policy is generally

The intuition is as follows. Let us assume that policymakers want to keep the unemployment rate below the natural rate. We further assume that the public has rational expectations. If both assumptions hold, then the public will know policymakers' motives and will raise their inflation expectations (i.e., in wage contracts) as a result.

However, we note that, even if agents have rational expectations, both information or nominal wage contract rigidities can lead to a temporary reduction in nominal wages and unemployment. These rigidities create an incentive for policymakers to violate any commitment to keep inflation stable.

Barro and Gordon (1983a, b) extend the Kydland and Prescott result to a multiperiod setting. However, even in this multiperiod setting (in which policymakers put a weight on future effects), there is no mechanism that ensures policymaker commitment to inflation stability.

conducted.[13] Furthermore, we assert that policymaker discretion need not be constrained by precommitment, but rather by well-known goals and guidelines (Leiderman and Svensson 1995; Bernanke et al. 1999; Albanesi et al. 2003). In this way, when policymakers act as dynamic programmers focused on specific goals and guidelines on how to meet those goals, policy can steer and then anchor public expectations. These goals and guidelines "tie down the price level [inflation] to a specific value at a given time" (Bernanke et al. 1999: 19).

Feature four follows from feature three. If policymaker discretion is influenced by specific guidelines, then this view of the policy process has implications for the variability trade-off between inflation and output (unemployment). Further, when policymakers act aggressively[14] to ensure

---

[13] See Chappell et al. (2005: 161–181) for a more supportive view that time consistency does permeate policymaker behavior.

[14] We note here that one policy indicator on which we rely throughout this book is the Taylor rule (1993a). The Taylor rule is a real short-term interest rate (under policymaker control). More specifically, the Taylor Rule is a linear function of the deviation of inflation from the policymakers inflation target, the deviation of output (unemployment) from its potential (natural) rate, and actual inflation.

The nontechnical use of the term *aggressive* refers to a policymaker's willingness to raise (lower) interest rates in response to explicit or implicit inflation target (output gap) deviations. In

efficient economic coordination, it is possible to reduce both inflation and output variability simultaneously. Hereafter, we refer to this outcome as *inflation-output costabilization (IOCS)*.[15] Our view is that ignoring the possibility of IOCS obscures the potential examination of alternative and beneficial policy actions or approaches. Trade-offs between inflation and output stability do exist, but the issue is not their existence, but when and why they occur. We argue that IOCS can occur under a policy framework that emphasizes inflation stability and information coordination.

A fifth feature is that, although a trade-off exists between inflation and output stability, there is also a feasible range of policy actions that encourage the simultaneous reduction in inflation and output volatility (IOCS). However, we do find a permanent trade-off between interest-rate volatility and IOCS.

The final feature is the coordination process itself and how it contributes to IOCS. We contend that when policymakers achieve and maintain inflation stability (usually by hitting

---

subsequent chapters we also use the term *aggressive* in relation to Taylor rule response parameters.

[15] The standard argument, which is summarized in Taylor (1979, 1994), shows there is a long-term trade-off between inflation and output (unemployment) variability.

prespecified targets), inflation volatility will not persist, because the public can (gradually) substitute the prespecified inflation target for past inflation. Within this economic environment, inflation and output stability can be encouraged because plans are now more certain. In the aggregate, plan stability reinforces inflation stability and output growing at its natural (or potential) rate. Consequently, a policy tack that stabilizes inflation reduces inflation persistence and contributes to IOCS.

1.2 Related Work

There is a very broad literature on the relation among politics, policy, and macroeconomic outcomes. Some of the general studies of the topic are by Alesina and Rosenthal (1995), Bernhard (2002), Drazen (2000), Franzese (2002), Iversen (1999), Morris (2000), Persson and Tabellini (2000), and Siklos (2002). These books deal with various policy issues, the effect of political institutions and rules, and (for some) the general area of macro political economy. Comprehensive works on policy and outcomes from a purely economic perspective can be found in Walsh (1998) and Woodford (2003). These two books take various topics and break them down into their constituent parts.

In contrast to these works, recall that we argue that the primary role of policymakers is to improve economic coordination. For the purposes of our theory, we treat policy as exogenous. Although endogenizing policy to economic, political, and social forces is an important avenue of research, we contend that the first priority is to establish a scientific explanation for policy effects. In doing so, we can establish a policymaker's role in coordinating (economic) information.

Our model is suited for a much more specific purpose: the relation between policy and the public. On a more technical level, our book also links formal and empirical analysis in a direct way. The books that have policy concerns akin to ours, as well as empirical tests, are Bryant et al. (1993) and Taylor (1993b). Our theoretical model shares related components – similar supply curve, an IS curve, and a policy rule – but we use the equilibria for different purposes. Because IOCS is a concern for us and a potentially important policy benefit, that is our focus. In contrast, Bryant et al. and Taylor's concerns are international, and their models are open where ours is closed.

We also differ with both Bryant et al. (1993) and Taylor (1993b) in how we model dynamics. We put an emphasis on adaptive learning and stability conditions that tie to structural outcomes, whereas they use more traditional methods.

Perhaps the book most closely related to how we model dynamics is Evans and Honkapohja (2001). Our book adapts the methods and practices they create in their book. However, their book is not empirical, but it does have EITM-like potential.

Our book is also related to work that has a policy (policymaker) and inflation focus at both the less technical (Leiderman and Svensson 1995; Blinder 1998; Bernanke et al. 1999) and more technical levels (Sargent 1999). On a practical policy level, our book is like Blinder's book in that we treat policymakers as dynamic programmers. Because we emphasize inflation stability and view implicit or explicit inflation targeting as one way to achieve this goal, we borrow from Leiderman and Svensson (1995) and Bernanke et al. (1999). Further, we use Bernanke et al.'s (1999) notion of policy frameworks.

Along with these particular policy aspects, our technical approach is similar to that of Sargent (1999). We model agent dynamics in a similar way and have a similar view of policy (although he tests rival hypotheses, some of which are related to time consistency).[16]

---

[16] Sargent's use of the concept of "self-confirming" equilibria involves a view of feedback and coordination that differs from ours. In Sargent's work, a *self-confirming equilibrium* is one in which

Despite these similarities, there are distinctions. First, the theoretical model we use places less emphasis on modeling strategic interaction and more emphasis on linking the policy effects to IOCS. Our model is in the tradition of dynamic macroeconomic models with no explicit game presented (see Rotemberg and Woodford 1997, 1998; McCallum 2001b). A second difference is that our priority is placed on the overall issue of coordination and not on time consistency concerns. To this end, we show that (price) information coordination can be achieved if policymakers assist the public in making more accurate inflation forecasts – to the point where the public substitutes an implicit or explicit inflation target for past values of inflation.

1.3 The Plan of the Book

This book is presented in three parts. Part I continues with a discussion and illustration of IOCS and policy. In Chapter 2 we present data related to IOCS and inflation uncertainty (information coordination). We find that IOCS has occurred in both the early to mid-1960s and since the mid-1980s.

"the government's beliefs about the Phillips curve affect its policy choices, which in turn makes agents act in such a way that the government's beliefs are confirmed" (p. 17).

These were periods of below-average volatility in inflation and output in the United States (Bullard 1998). Inflation uncertainty is less during periods of IOCS as well. Our findings, which use surveyed inflation expectations data, suggest that periods of greater economic coordination occur *during* IOCS periods. We find that inflation forecast errors decrease in volatility during IOCS periods as well.

Chapter 2 also relates policy actions to IOCS.[17] Using various policy indicators, we find that inflation-stabilizing policy[18] occurs during IOCS periods. We also find a trade-off between IOCS and interest rate volatility. In Chapter 3 we use a historical-narrative approach to examine the evolution of scientific doctrine and how it and economic events in-

---

[17] We assume policymakers influence, via open market operations (see Bernanke and Blinder 1992), the real rate of interest to change output (unemployment) relative to the potential (natural) rate. The Taylor rule demonstrates that policymakers' responses to inflation target deviations will influence the gap between actual and potential (natural) output (unemployment). Note that the traditional explanation is that inflation stability is achieved at the expense of output stability. Our view is that IOCS is achieved at the expense of interest rate stability.

[18] One inflation-stabilizing policy tack is to apply the Taylor principle. The intuition behind the Taylor principle is that the monetary authority should raise (lower) *real* interest rates in response to higher (lower) rates of inflation. A more technical treatment follows in subsequent chapters.

fluenced implementation of inflation-stabilizing policy and, ultimately, IOCS. We find that large differences in policy response to surges in inflation or deviations from an implicit inflation target (as measured by interest rate responses in the last 40 years) coincide with changes in scientific doctrine.

The historical analysis, although only suggestive, indicates a consistent relation between the belief in a structural Phillips curve (the slope) and implementation of an inflation-stabilizing policy. We find, for example, that responses to inflation instability have been much more aggressive in the past 20 years. This finding is consistent with the more recent scientific view that there is no long-term trade-off between inflation and unemployment (output).

Part II of the book centers on how the implementation of inflation-stabilizing policy influences aggregate volatility. In Chapter 4 we present a simple macroeconomic model that allows us to evaluate policy effects. The model is standard in the macroeconomic literature and provides a foundation for the theoretical results in the ensuing chapters. (For background information, see Brainard 1967; Bomfim 1997; McCallum 2001b; Kimura and Kurozumi (2003.)

We explore in Chapter 5 the possible trade-offs posed by various policy targets (goals) (Blinder 1998: 3) and how different policy target mixes (interest rate responses) affect the stochastic behavior of the business cycle. Chapter 5 also pays particular attention to our policy rule choice. A policy rule expresses the monetary authorities' policy instrument based on their goals and the available information. Our choice for use of a particular policy rule follows from the work of Bryant et al. (1993) and Taylor (1993b). They argue that the best policy rules produce desirable results in a variety of competing macroeconomic environments. Based on their criteria, we use a contemporaneous-information Taylor rule.

Using the Taylor rule, we then show that aggressive inflation-stabilizing policy is consistent with reductions in inflation and output volatility. In Chapter 5 we solve the model and examine the policy (goal/objective) trade-offs (Blinder 1998: 3, 54) by focusing on marginal rates of substitution between the target variables – inflation and output (see Svensson 2003a). We refer to these effects as the *crossover effects of output targeting (CEOT)* and the *crossover effects of inflation targeting (CEIT)*.

In Chapter 6 we use a simple policymaker loss function to show that the optimal policymaker role is to be aggressive in stabilizing both inflation and output. We find that when greater weight is assigned to stabilizing inflation, it is possible to reduce simultaneously the instability of both inflation and output (i.e., IOCS).

Using some traditional evaluation procedures, the results indicate, even after accounting for crossover effects, that there is a feasible range for aggressive policy responses consistent with a simultaneous reduction in inflation and output volatility. We also find a trade-off between interest rate volatility and IOCS (see Fuhrer and Moore 1995b).

Part III shifts focus from macroeconomic effects to the relation between policymakers and the public – coordination dynamics. In Chapter 7, we use the empirical implications of our theoretical model (EITM) and forge a link between the formal model and the empirical test. We find that when policymakers achieve and maintain inflation stability (usually by hitting prespecified targets), inflation will not persist.[19] Inflation will also become less volatile. We argue that the intuition behind this result is that the public learns the policymakers' inflation target and uses that target (and

---

[19] See Rudd and Whelan (2003) on why many small-scale models fail to account for inflation persistence. Without an accounting for how policy can influence inflation persistence, it is difficult to see how policy can assist in IOCS outcomes.

gradually replaces past inflation behavior) for its inflation expectations.[20]

In Chapter 8 we show that the condition for determinacy and learnability for the rational expectations equilibrium (REE) occurs when policymakers respond more aggressively to inflation target deviations.[21] This finding provides a stronger argument in favor of the robustness of aggressive inflation-stabilizing policy – and the avoidance of deflationary outcomes.

Chapter 9 presents our conclusions. If our theory and results are accurate, then the coordinated transmission of economic information requires policymakers to engage in aggressive inflation-stabilizing policies. To a lesser extent, policymakers should work to stabilize output as well, but not at the expense of inflation stability. We also explore ways to extend our findings. We contend that it is important

[20] These results can be generalized to situations in which the public has heterogeneous expectations (Kandel and Zilberfarb 1999; Owyang and Ramey 2002; Granato and Wong 2005).

[21] McCallum (2002a, b, 2003) suggests that an aggressive inflation-stabilizing policy can produce either explosive and unlearnable or stable and learnable equilibria. Forward-looking models such as Woodford's (1999) could produce explosive and unlearnable results. On the other hand, models that include past information produce stable and learnable equilibria.

to examine the robustness of our findings by doing a comparative-nation (institutional), open-economy analysis. We also think the model could be revised to include the potential political and social forces that influence the role of policymakers.

— ✦ **CHAPTER TWO** ✦ —

Outcomes and Policy: An Illustration

Periods of serious price disturbances are periods of industrial and financial disturbance and social unrest. Practically never one without the other. And periods of price stability are periods of industrial and social equilibrium and sanity.

Carl Snyder (1935: 202)

A central concept in this book is the simultaneous decline in inflation and output volatility – inflation-output costabilization (IOCS). Many researchers have documented the decline in economic volatility in the United States and elsewhere (Kim and Nelson 1999; McConnell and Perez-Quiros 2000; Blanchard and Simon 2001; Kahn, McConnell, and Perez-Quiros 2001, 2002; Labhard 2003; Martin and Rowthorn 2004). Much of this work focuses on output stability. One consistent finding is that this work dates the decline in volatility to the 1980s.

In this chapter we extend this research in several ways. Our purpose is to illustrate the economic stability in the United States since the 1980s and lay the groundwork for the relation between IOCS and policy. We explore this linkage in the following manner. First, we investigate the behavior of economic data. In particular, we examine together (and then separately) the volatility of inflation and output. Our particular concern, of course, is IOCS – the simultaneous and sustained reduction of both inflation and output volatility.[1] In addition, to see if periods of inflation and output stability occur prior to the 1980s, our analysis covers the period 1960–2000. Finally, because we contend that IOCS depends on the coordination of price information, we examine the ability of the public to make and learn correct inflation forecasts. We determine if inflation forecast accuracy and stability coincide with periods of IOCS.

This chapter then illustrates the relation between policy and these outcomes. The issue is to determine whether policymakers took actions at similar times that enhanced the coordination of price information and thereby reduced inflation uncertainty during periods of IOCS. We demonstrate

---

[1] We assess inflation and output volatility by using the standard deviation of the consumer price index (CPI; rate of change) and real GDP (growth rate), respectively.

this relation by connecting the policy indicators to inflation-stabilizing policy and IOCS for the period 1960–2000.

This connection between inflation-stabilizing policy and IOCS also points to an alternative trade-off. We illustrate that the real trade-off is not between inflation and output volatility, but between interest rate volatility and IOCS. The reason is that aggressive implementation of the Taylor rule (applying the Taylor principle) can lead to large, rapid swings in interest (short- and long-term) rates. In other words, inflation-stabilization policies create added volatility in interest rates, even though this policy tack coordinates public inflation expectations and encourages IOCS.

2.1 Inflation-Output Costabilization: The Data

We use Bullard's (1998) measures of inflation (percentage change in the CPI) and output (real GDP growth) volatility.[2] The two series are 21-quarter (five-year), centered, moving

---

[2] The centered-moving standard deviation is calculated as follows:

$$\sigma_{X_t} = \sqrt{\frac{\Sigma_{\tau=\frac{2t-s+1}{2}}^{\frac{2t+s-1}{2}} \left(X_\tau - \bar{X}_t\right)^2}{s-1}}$$

standard deviations.[3] Zero signifies the average for the entire series. Using these series, we argue that IOCS occurs when both the inflation and output series exhibit below-average volatility. The correlation between the two series is 0.73. Figure 2.1 shows that IOCS occurs between 1962:I–1970:I and 1984:III–2000:I.

As a robustness check and to see whether IOCS is not an artifact of the periodicity of the moving standard deviation, we estimate two alternative periods: 17-quarter (four-year) and 25-quarter (six-year). We find that this adjustment does not significantly alter the dates when IOCS occurs. Roughly speaking, for all three time frames, IOCS occurs in two different periods: 1962–9 and 1985–2000. We also find (using Figure 2.1) that during the 41-year period, only in 4 years or portions thereof (1960, 1961, 1970, 1984) do the two series have opposite movements in volatility.

and

$$\bar{X}_t = \frac{\sum_{\tau=\frac{2t-s+1}{2}}^{\frac{2t+s-1}{2}} X_\tau}{s}, \text{ for } X_t \in \{\pi_t, y_t\}$$

where s is the length of the rolling windows.

[3] Note that these types of data transformations create some persistence and "push forward" some effects of the past, which affects the precision of dating specific events, particularly in the transition from one state to another.

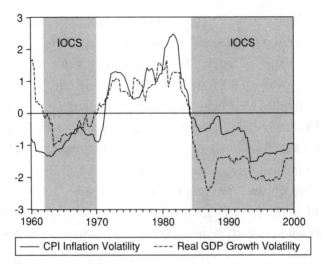

Figure 2.1 *IOCS, 1960–2000 (5-year moving standard deviation). Note: Data are from Bullard (1998). The data are transformed to 21-quarter (5-year) moving standard deviations for the CPI inflation rate and real GDP growth. The zero line indicates the average for each series. Shaded areas represent periods of IOCS (1962:I–1970:I and 1984:III–2000:I).*

2.1.1 Inflation Volatility

In Figure 2.1, above-average inflation volatility occurred during the 1971–85 period. Further examination shows that inflation volatility started increasing in 1971 and that this volatility peaked in 1983. In 1983, volatility started to drop precipitously and has stayed below average since 1985.

In Table 2.1 we categorize inflation volatility by decade. Consistent with Figure 2.1, the 1960s and 1990s were the least volatile decades. The mean volatility for these two decades was −0.92 and −1.04, respectively, indicating that both decades were below average for the sample. The 1970s and 1980s both had above-average inflation volatility (0.73 and 0.50, respectively). However, the volatility in the 1980s was not the same as the 1970s. During the 1970s inflation trended upward, peaking in the early 1980s. On the other hand, in the early 1980s the inflation trend was downward, with some added volatility during the transition to lower inflation.

Table 2.1 also shows that these differences among decades are, for the most part, statistically distinct. Comparing prior and successive decades, we find that the mean level of inflation volatility for the 1960s was statistically different from that of the 1970s and that the 1980s level was different from that of the 1990s. On the other hand, the 1970s and 1980s levels were statistically the same, but this result is due to the similarity between the early 1980s and the 1970s.

We also find that breaking down the data by IOCS periods (1962:I–1970:I; 1984:III–2000:I) and non-IOCS periods (1970:II–1984:II) shows statistically distinct patterns in inflation volatility. Using IOCS/non-IOCS period breakdowns,

Table 2.1. *Inflation Volatility*

	Time Period				
	1960–9	1970–9	1980–9	1990–9	1960–2001
Mean	−0.92	0.73	0.50	−1.04	−0.18
t-statistics of Mean Equality (*p*-value in parentheses)	14.25 (0.00)	1.08 (0.27)		8.13 (0.00)	
Standard Deviation	0.30	0.67	1.14	0.35	1.06
F-statistics of Variance Equality (*p*-value in parenthesis)	4.98 (0.00)	2.93 (0.00)		10.73 (0.00)	

Note: The *t*- and F-tests for mean and variance equality are between the current and successive decade (1960–9 compared to 1970–9, 1970–9 compared to 1980–9, 1980–9 compared to 1990–9). Data are Bullard's (1998) 21-quarter (5-year) moving standard deviations for the CPI.

we find the mean inflation volatility for 1962:I–1970:I was −0.88, 1.04 for 1970:II–1984:II, and −0.82 for 1984:III–2000:I. Tests for mean equality (not reported in Table 2.1) indicate that the mean level of inflation volatility is statistically different between the IOCS and non-IOCS periods.[4] However, we do not find a significant statistical difference between the two IOCS periods.[5]

2.1.2 Output Volatility

Table 2.2 categorizes output volatility by decade. Consistent with Figure 2.1, Table 2.2 shows that below-average volatility occurred in every decade except the 1970s. The 1990s was by far the least volatile decade. The 1980s exhibited the beginning of a sharp decline that was sustained in the 1990s.

We also find that the 1980s and 1990s were the least volatile decades. The mean volatility for these two decades was −0.43 and −1.74, respectively, indicating that both decades

---

[4] A difference of means test shows statistically significant differences in inflation volatility:
  - 1962:I–1970:I compared to 1970:II–1984:II (t-test $= 12.22$; p-value $= 0.00$).
  - 1970:II–1984:II compared to 1984:III–2000:I (t-test $= 15.25$; p-value $= 0.00$).

[5] The t-test for 1962:I–1970:I compared to 1984:III–2000:I is 0.51 (p-value $= 0.61$).

were below average for the sample. The 1970s had above-average output volatility (0.74).

Table 2.2 also shows that these differences among decades are statistically distinct. Comparing prior and successive decades, we find that the mean level of output volatility of the 1960s was statistically different from that of the 1970s, the mean level of the 1970s differed from that of the 1980s, and the 1980s mean level was different from that of the 1990s.

We also find that breaking down the data by IOCS (1962:I–1970:I; 1984:III–2000:I) and non-IOCS (1970:II–1984:II) periods shows statistically distinct patterns in output volatility. Using IOCS/non-IOCS period breakdowns, we find the mean output volatility for 1962–9 was −0.47, 0.78 for 1970:II–1984:II, and −1.73 for 1984:III–2000:I.

Tests for mean equality (not reported in Table 2.2) indicate that the mean level of output volatility is statistically different between the IOCS and non-IOCS periods and also between the two IOCS periods.[6] We also find a

---

[6] A difference of means test finds statistically significant differences in output volatility:

- 1962:I–1970:I compared to 1970:II–1984:II (t-test $= 13.60$; p-value $= 0.00$).
- 1970:II–1984:II compared to 1984:III–2000:I (t-test $= 33.31$; p-value $= 0.00$).

Table 2.2. *Output Volatility*

	Time Period				
	1960–9	1970–9	1980–9	1990–9	1960–2001
Mean	−0.22	0.74	−0.43	−1.74	−0.42
t-statistics of Mean Equality	8.39	5.16	5.74		
(p-value in parenthesis)	(0.00)	(0.00)	(0.00)		
Standard Deviation	0.63	0.35	1.40	0.30	1.19
F-statistics of Variance Equality	3.17	15.36	21.03		
(p-value in parenthesis)	(0.00)	(0.00)	(0.00)		

Note: The *t*- and F-tests for mean and variance equality are between the current and successive decades (1960–9 compared to 1970–9, 1970–9 compared to 1980–9, 1980–9 compared to 1990–9). Data are Bullard's (1998) 21-quarter (5-year) moving standard deviations for real GDP growth.

significant statistical difference during the two IOCS periods.[7]

Taken as a whole, these tests show statistically distinct patterns in behavior in both inflation and output volatility and in IOCS. These data suggest that, when categorized by decade, inflation volatility is at its highest during the 1970s and early 1980s and output volatility is highest during the 1970s. We also find that when we break down the data by IOCS and non-IOCS periods, the categorization has statistical power. The IOCS and non-IOCS periods are statistically different for both inflation and output volatility. The IOCS periods have less inflation and output volatility. These statistical tests add further weight to the IOCS/non-IOCS breakdown shown in Figure 2.1.

One added finding from the statistical results is that, although the two IOCS periods are statistically similar when it comes to inflation volatility, the later IOCS period, 1984:III–2000:I, has a statistically different output volatility pattern. Output volatility is low in the 1962:I–1970:I period, but it is even lower in the 1984:III–2000:I period. This finding conforms with the growing consensus that, beginning

---

[7] The t-test for 1962:I–1970:I compared to 1984:III–2000:I is 17.48 (p-value $= 0.00$).

in the early 1980s, there was a shift toward greater output stability.

2.1.3 Data on Inflation Uncertainty

There have been debates about how to diagnose the threats to economic stability and the ways that policy could achieve economic stability. Prior work and thought about policy and business cycles focused on how the public could be influenced by policy. There was and is a belief that public expectations are endogenous to policy (see Bernanke et al. 1999: 266–270). If this relation holds, then policy could work to coordinate information so that expectations could be correct on average.

We asserted in Chapter 1 that when policymakers act aggressively to stabilize inflation, they encourage efficient economic coordination (see Ball and Romer 2003). We also asserted that, when policymakers achieve and maintain inflation stability (usually by hitting prespecified targets), inflation volatility will not persist, because the public can substitute the prespecified inflation target for past inflation.

In the aggregate, the predictive stability that current plans now possess translates into inflation stability and output growth at its natural rate. Within this economic environment, inflation stability and output stability can be sustained (up to a point) because the plans exhibit greater (price) stability. The linkage therefore flows from policy to inflation stability to IOCS.

In this section we explore the changes in inflation expectations and relate them to the changes in IOCS. We expect a negative relation between the size of inflation forecast errors and the periods of IOCS.

Inflation expectations surveys were conducted by the Survey Research Center (SRC) at the University of Michigan, and the results were published in the *Survey of Consumer Attitudes*. Survey respondents were asked approximately 50 core questions that covered three broad areas of consumer opinion: personal finances, business conditions, and buying conditions. We used the following two questions that relate to measuring inflation expectations:

1. During the next 12 months, do you think that prices in general will go up, or go down, or stay where they are now?

2. By about what percent do you expect prices to go (up/down), on the average, during the next 12 months?

If respondents expected the price level would go up (or down) on question 1, they were asked in the second question to provide the exact percentage the price level would increase (or decrease); otherwise, the second question was coded as 0 percent.[8]

The survey of individual inflation forecasts (one year ahead) shows a pattern that is similar to actual changes in the overall inflation rate. Inflation forecasts began their upward movement in 1968 and moved in a cyclical, but upward trend. This trend peaked in 1981. Figure 2.2 also indicates that there was far greater volatility in forecasts starting in the late 1960s, which only receded in the mid-1980s.

In Table 2.3 we categorize surveyed inflation expectations by decade. Consistent with Figure 2.2, the 1970s had the highest average forecast. The mean forecast for the 1970s was 6.78, which is above average for the sample (4.81). Table 2.3 shows that the differences among decades are statistically distinct. When we compare prior and successive decades, we find that the mean inflation forecast of the 1960s was statistically different from the 1970s, the 1970s'

---

[8] Some respondents might have confused the concepts of change in level and change in rate. To account for this confusion, respondents who answered "stay the same" on question 1 were asked the following to eliminate any confusion: "Do you mean that prices will go up at the same rate as now, or that prices in general will not go up during the next 12 months?" For more details on the surveying procedures, see http://www.sca.isr.umich.edu/.

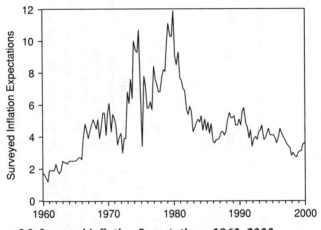

Figure 2.2 Surveyed Inflation Expectations, 1960–2000.
Note: Data in this sample are quarterly and are provided by the University of Michigan (SRC) "Surveys of Consumers" (http:// www. sca.isr.umich.edu/), Table 19. For further details, see Section 2.1.3 of this book.

forecast differed from that of the 1980s, and the forecast of the 1980s differed from that of the 1990s.

Not surprisingly, inflation forecast errors show a volatility pattern similar to that of the forecasts. Figure 2.3 shows that inflation forecast errors became noticeably more volatile beginning in 1970 and that this volatility was sustained until the mid-1980s. What is also interesting is that most forecast errors were negative; that is, individuals forecasted higher

Table 2.3. *Surveyed Inflation Expectations*

	Time Period				
	1960–9	1970–9	1980–9	1990–9	1960–2001
Mean	3.07	6.78	5.47	3.95	4.81
t-statistics of Mean Equality (*p*-value in parenthesis)	9.16 (0.00)	2.93 (0.00)	5.01 (0.00)		
Standard Deviation	1.28	2.21	1.76	0.71	2.12
F-statistics of Variance Equality (*p*-value in parenthesis)	2.96 (0.00)	1.56 (0.16)	6.07 (0.00)		

Note: The *t*- and F-tests for mean and variance equality are between the current and successive decades (1960–9 compared to 1970–9, 1970–9 compared to 1980–9, 1980–9 compared to 1990–9). Data in this sample are quarterly and are provided by the University of Michigan (SRC) "Surveys of Consumers" (http://www.sca.isr.umich.edu/), Table 19. For further details, see Section 2.1.3 of this book.

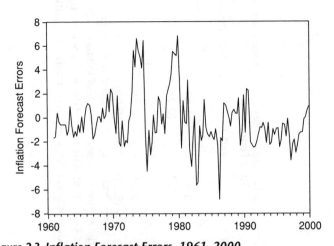

Figure 2.3 *Inflation Forecast Errors, 1961–2000.*
Note: See note to Figure 2.2. These data show the difference between the actual inflation rate (CPI) and the surveyed inflation expectations (Figure 2.2) for that date. CPI data are provided by the Federal Reserve Bank of St. Louis (FRED II), and are available at http://research.stlouisfed.org/fred2/.

inflation than actually occurred. The exception to this was the decade of the 1970s.

In Table 2.4 we categorize inflation forecast error by decade. We find the lowest mean forecast error occurred in the 1960s (−0.17), and the highest was in the 1970s (1.28) and 1990s (−1.27), although the 1970s and 1990s had errors of opposite signs. The average for the sample was −0.31.

Table 2.4. *Inflation Forecast Error*

	Time Period				
	1960–9	1970–9	1980–9	1990–9	1960–2001
Mean	−0.17	1.28	−0.87	−1.27	−0.31
t-statistics of Mean Equality	2.72	3.54	1.07		
(*p*-value in parenthesis)	(0.00)	(0.00)	(0.28)		
Standard Deviation	1.11	3.20	2.13	1.03	2.25
F-statistics of Variance Equality	8.20	2.24	4.29		
(*p*-value in parenthesis)	(0.00)	(0.01)	(0.00)		

Note: See note to Table 2.3. These data are the difference between the actual inflation rate (CPI) and the surveyed inflation expectations (Table 2.3) for that date. CPI data are provided by the Federal Reserve Bank of St. Louis (FRED II), and are available at http://research.stlouisfed.org/fred2/.

The standard deviation gives a better sense of the absolute forecast error, which was highest during the 1970s and early 1980s. However, again, this result was caused by the sustained increase in inflation during the 1970s and the sustained decline in inflation that started in the early 1980s.

Another issue was the sustained overprediction during the 1980s and 1990s. There could be many reasons for this, ranging from institutional to psychological and historical (i.e., the Fisher Effect). What is striking about this "premium" is that it held at about 1.0 to 1.5 percent from the mid–1990s onward.

Table 2.4 also shows that these differences among decades are, for the most part, statistically distinct. Comparing prior and successive decades, we find that the mean inflation forecast error of the 1960s was statistically different from that of the 1970s, and the error of the 1970s was different from that of the 1980s. On the other hand, the mean inflation forecast errors of the 1980s and 1990s were statistically the same.

We also find that breaking down the data by IOCS (1962:I–1970:I; 1984:III–2000:I) and non-IOCS (1970:II–1984:II) periods shows statistically distinct patterns in forecast errors. Using IOCS/non-IOCS period breakdowns, we find the mean inflation forecast error for 1962:1–1970:I was −0.04, 0.37 for 1970:II–1984:II, and −0.92 for 1984:III–2000:I.

Tests for mean equality (not reported in Table 2.4) indicate that the mean level of inflation forecast error is statistically different between the later IOCS period (1984:III–2000:I) and the first IOCS period (1962:I–1970:I) and between the later IOCS period and the non-IOCS period (1970:II–1984:II).[9] There is no statistical difference between the first IOCS period and the non-IOCS period.[10]

We note that the public's uncertainty about inflation is not isolated; it also extends to policymakers. Romer and Romer (2002) examine the Fed Greenbook forecasts since 1967 and arrive at the following conclusion:

In the late 1960s and early 1970s, the average forecast error (calculated as actual inflation minus the forecasted value) was substantially positive. That is, the forecasts substantially underpredicted inflation in this

[9] The difference of means test finds statistically significant differences in forecast errors:

- 1962:I–1970:I compared to 1984:III–2000:I (t-test $= 2.83$; p-value $= 0.00$)
- 1970:II–1984:II compared to 1984:III–2000:I (t-test $= 2.9$; p-value $= 0.00$)

[10] The t-test for 1962:I–1970:I compared to 1970:II–1984:II is 0.72 (p-value $= 0.47$).

period. The average error was 1.2 percentage points in the late Martin and early Burns period (1967: 10 to 1975: 6). In both the Volcker and Greenspan eras, the average forecast error was small and slightly negative (−0.4 percentage points and −0.3 percentage points, respectively). Thus, in contrast to the forecasts for the 1960s and 1970s, the modern Greenbook forecasts have, if anything, tended to overpredict inflation. The bias in the forecasts exhibits interesting fluctuations in the 1970s. The forecasts became dramatically less positively biased in the middle of the decade (p. 43).

Thus far in this chapter, we have examined and illustrated macroeconomic stability and instability in the United States since 1960. We find that both inflation and output stability (IOCS) coexisted for a large part of this 41-year period. In particular, IOCS occurred for the periods 1962–9 and 1985–2000, periods that coincide with the longest business expansions since 1854.

Because IOCS depends on the coordination of price information, we also study the ability of the public to make and learn correct inflation forecasts. We analyze the increasing inflation forecast accuracy and volatility to see if they coincide with periods of IOCS. Between 1970 and the mid-1980s, we find inflation forecast errors are the most volatile and that it takes time for the public to learn the equilibrium inflation rate. We note that this inflation uncertainty was also shared by policymakers (Romer and Romer 2002).[11]

2.2 Inflation-Stabilization Policy and IOCS

At the beginning of this chapter, we presented data illustrating the existence of IOCS. Decreases in both inflation and output volatility can occur simultaneously. We also found that inflation forecast stability accompanied the two recent expansions.[12] On the other hand, between the economic expansions of the early to mid-1960s and the 1980s and the 1990s came the stagflation of the 1970s. Between 1965 and 1980, inflation went through three cycles (1967–1968, 1973–1974, and 1978–1979), with each cycle being more volatile than the previous one. Unemployment and output

[11] The fact that U.S. output growth is more stable now than it was between 1970 and early 1980 has important implications in interpreting policy-relevant data. In non-IOCS periods a change in output growth could be (mis)interpreted as noise caused by the volatility. During IOCS periods, a similar change would be more likely to be interpreted accurately and lead to an optimal policy response. In terms of policy implementation IOCS periods can give policymakers added freedom to pursue preemptive policies – something that was done in the 1990s (see Chapter 3).

[12] The data show that the three longest economic expansions, peacetime or otherwise (since 1854), coincided with inflation stability.

follow a similar pattern of increasing volatility during these inflationary times.

This section of Chapter 2 builds on these findings and explores the relation between inflation-stabilizing policy and IOCS. Underlying this analysis is a concern about how the public reacts to certain policy stances and how it uses them to reduce its uncertainty about current and future inflation. Although inflation-stabilizing policy practices are influenced by political, social, and institutional factors,[13] we focus our analysis on the effects of inflation-stabilizing monetary policy.

In this section we first present a description of how policymakers coordinate economic information by implementing policies designed to stabilize inflation. We characterize policy as akin to dynamic programming, in which policymakers respond to new information as it arises.

To take this dynamic programming analogy further, we think a policy framework can be characterized, in part, as a rule – a contingency plan – to deal with the sequence of information, subject to some goal or target. A general targeting rule specifies the objectives to be achieved and lists

---

[13] We do allude to these influences in Chapter 3, but they are not central to our theory. Our focus is on the influence and role that policymakers play, not on the sources of policymaker action.

the target variables (or forecasts of these variables) and the levels that are to be achieved.[14]

Recall, however, that the sequential nature of policy – treating policy as a dynamic programming problem – creates an incentive to lower unemployment or increase output by generating a greater-than-expected inflation[15] (Sargent 2002). The time-consistency "problem" shows that, absent explicit constraints on policymaker discretion, any policy rule is not credible (Kydland and Prescott 1977; Barro and Gordon 1983a, b).

However, it is far from clear whether time consistency is more than a cautionary theoretical footnote. Blinder (1998: 40–43) notes that this inflation bias induced by time inconsistency is not a very robust result.[16] The disinflations and even the deflations that occurred in the 1980s suggest that there is no inflation bias. Another more technical point is

---

[14] We argue that it is better to respond to current inflation and output target/gap deviations than to one target deviation alone (Rudebusch and Svensson 1999; Svensson 2003a). However, we will argue for an *added* emphasis on inflation stabilization. We explore these issues of relative target (gap) response in greater detail in the Parts II and III.

[15] See Chapter 1, Footnote 12.

[16] For a technical treatment that casts doubt on the overall robustness of the time consistency-inflation bias relation, see Albanesi et al. (2003). For a more sympathetic treatment, see Ireland (1999).

that the theoretical basis for the inflation bias fails to hold up (in most models) when parameter values in the policy-maker loss functions for the natural rate of unemployment are not of a specific magnitude.

We acknowledge that time consistency is an important theoretical possibility, but we choose to focus on known policy rule characteristics that help show how policy co-ordinates public information streams. Doing so requires aggressive implementation of the Taylor rule or some related general targeting rule. We use several policy indicators, including a policy rule (related to the real interest rate), to determine if there is a consistent movement in policy and whether it is toward or away from inflation stabilization. Our indicators rely on alternative representations of a short-term interest rate.

2.2.1 Policymakers and Information Coordination

How does countercyclical policy coordinate public inflation expectations? We assert that a policymaker serves a function similar to that of a Walrasian auctioneer (Walras 1874/ 1954; Leijonhufvud 1968). Walras argues that market processes are coordinated by a fictional auctioneer. The auctioneer facilitates market exchanges between buyer and seller by calling out various prices. Buyers and sellers then react to the called-out price through the sequence of sales and purchases. As this process continues and new prices are called out, eventually all buyers and sellers will settle on the "market" price.

The Walrasian general equilibrium has an important social and economic property in that it is efficient. In other words, it is not feasible to increase output (holding input fixed) or to decrease inputs (holding output fixed) without reducing the utility of someone (see Katzner 1989). Although we argue markets do eventually clear, we also think there are coordination failures in which mutual gains go unrealized.[17] Further, we argue that it is the uncoordinated inflation expectations of agents that are the primary cause of the coordination failure. Here we see the role of a policymaker as akin to a Walrasian auctioneer. Policymakers do not typically call out what price inflation is and will be in the future, but their actions can minimize the public's inflation expectation uncertainty. By reducing uncertainty over the current and future inflation rate, policymakers reduce the risk of coordination problems.

---

[17] See Barro and Grossman (1976) for modifications of the Walrasian framework.

To help isolate this coordination effect, we treat the policymaker as an exogenous actor. We are interested in the consequences of what policymakers do, rather than why they do it. Recall our viewpoint that the relationship between policymakers and the public is dynamic. This dynamic framework involves thinking about policy as a choice of action to which policymakers commit for some length of time. A dynamic emphasis enables us to look at times when policy changed and what the consequences were.

The public's relationship with policymakers centers on its choosing a contingency plan for current and future variables under its control. These plans include the public's future assessments of the policy rule. A key issue in the public's assessment of policy is demonstrating how the public learns the policy. It is here that the specific coordination effect occurs, because policy can stabilize key variables (inflation) about which the public has expectations. In stabilizing these variables, policymakers remove uncertainty and expedite learning on the part of the public.[18]

---

[18] Recent work on learning models assumes that the public updates as if it were using regressions on endogenous data to form its expectations. When it does so, under certain conditions (E-stability), it learns the REE. This approach is demonstrated in Chapters 7 and 8.

We assume that learning is a local concept, which means policymakers can help the public learn the "correct" equilibrium (i.e., the REE). Because the choice of the policy rule influences the equilibrium information set, this choice determines the learnability properties of any equilibrium. In this case, the equilibrium will be the policymakers' (implicit or explicit) inflation target.

2.3 Policy Indicators

Policy is a plan or action, and policy instruments are the mechanisms that policymakers alter to achieve policy goals. These policy instruments can affect the real interest rate. Moreover, temporary price rigidities in the economy provide friction that gives rise to policy (real interest rate) effects on aggregate demand and inflation expectations. We also think that monetary policy implementation, informed by the natural rate hypothesis and rational expectations, provides the limits of feasible countercyclical policy (see, for example, Chung 1990; Sargent 1999; Clarida, Gali, and Gertler 2000). Under such theoretical constraints, inflation stabilizing policy assists in stabilizing business cycle fluctuations.

Policymakers can influence real interest rates through the manipulation of short-term interest rates. For empirical policy studies in the United States, the short-term interest rate under policymaker influence is typically the federal funds rate (i_t^f).[19] This policy instrument has known links to private credit markets. Stock and Watson (1988) find that the federal funds rate has a long-term statistical relation to three-month and one-year Treasury bill rates. These Treasury-bill rates compete with market interest rates. The federal funds rate also has long-term implications. The expectations theory of the term structure of interest rates tells us that longer-term interest rates are expectations of future short-term rates.

With this in mind, we use the following indicators (see also Brunner and Meltzer 1969). What they share is a relation to the federal funds rate (and real interest rates).

- the federal funds rate ratio
- the Taylor rule (Taylor principle)
- Taylor principle deviations (and volatility)

---

[19] The federal funds rate is the interest rate that banks with excess reserves at a Federal Reserve district bank charge other banks that need overnight loans.

2.3.1 The Federal Funds Rate Ratio

The federal funds rate ratio is our simplest policy indicator. The federal funds rate is generally regarded as a key operating target for monetary policy. It is influenced by exogenous variables, such as money demand and inflation expectations, but it is affected most directly and most immediately by open market operations (Bernanke and Blinder 1992).

Yet, the federal funds rate itself is not an adequate indicator for inflation stabilization. Like all interest rate indicators, it is subject to the interest rate fallacy. As Friedman (1969) has noted, one must be careful in interpreting low (high) interest rates as being a sign of a loose (tight) policy because, after accounting for liquidity and price effects, low (high) interest rates can also signal tight (loose) monetary policy.

To extend the interest rate fallacy further, the federal funds rate does not tell us the degree to which the policymakers attack inflation nor does it indicate how policymakers maintain this policy stance to support positive real rates of return on investment and savings. In short, federal funds rate increases do not necessarily mean that policy has moved to an inflation-stabilizing policy stance.

We could rely on the *real* federal funds rate as a policy indicator, because it would signify the price for deferring consumption (Breeden 1979) and would also influence the term structure and the yield curve. However, a real interest rate can be a misleading indicator of policy direction because it cannot be compared across time periods. For example, if we compare policy in the 1960s with policy in the 1980s, we find large differences in real rates, suggesting different policies toward inflation stability. Yet, we also know from historical accounts (Stein 1994; DeLong 1997; Orphanides 2003) and estimates of the Taylor rule (Taylor 1999a; Clarida et al. 2000; Mehra 2002) that, for part of the 1960s and nearly all of the 1980s, monetary policy was trying to maintain inflation stability.[20]

For comparability across time periods we combine the log of the ratio of the federal funds rate (i_t^f) with the annual inflation rate, $\log(i_t^f/\pi_t)$, to arrive at the federal funds rate ratio (Granato 1996). Because the scale is logarithmic, equal proportions are shown as equal distances, which allows for greater comparability across time periods.[21] Moreover, the federal funds rate ratio is related to other

---

[20] Other indicators could be used, such as the ex-ante federal funds rate or Federal Reserve Greenbook predictions (Romer and Romer 2002).

[21] For example, if i_t/π_t changed from 1 to 2, its distance is equivalent to a change from 2 to 4.

macroeconomic indicators of interest (i.e., the Taylor principle).

Inflation Stabilization and the Federal Funds Rate Ratio. We argue that the federal funds rate ratio signifies an inflation-stabilizing policy emphasis when it is greater than or equal to unity. Because the scale is logarithmic, the condition $\log\left(i_t^f/\pi_t\right) \geq 0$ is analogous to the Taylor principle. On the other hand, a negative value on this logarithmic scale is consistent with a policy stance that deemphasizes inflation stability.

Figure 2.4 depicts the federal funds rate ratio for the period 1960–2000. The figure shows several features of inflation stability. Inflation stability was deemphasized during the period 1974 to 1980 (shaded area). There was a slight shift toward an inflation-stabilizing emphasis in 1978 $\left(\log\left(i_t^f/\pi_t\right) = 0.04\right)$, but it was against the overall trend.

The federal funds rate ratio also showed a distinct pattern of declining resolve in maintaining an inflation-stabilizing policy. This pattern started in 1966 and was not reversed until 1981, when inflation-stabilizing policy reasserted itself and continued to the year 2000. In 1993, monetary policy responded to an economic slowdown by becoming expansionary, but the ratio still did not fall below zero

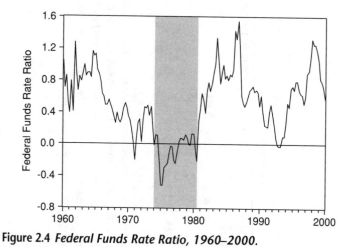

Figure 2.4 *Federal Funds Rate Ratio, 1960–2000.*
Note: This variable is the log of the ratio of the federal funds rate to the annual inflation rate (CPI). Data are quarterly. The federal funds rate and CPI data are provided by the Federal Reserve Bank of St. Louis (FRED II), and are available at http://research. stlouisfed.org/fred2/. The zero line indicates that the federal funds rate and the inflation rate are equal. Shaded area represents 1974:I–1980:III.

$\left(\log \left(i_t^f / \pi_t \right) = 0.01 \right)$. This drop was consistent with the aggressive inflation-stabilizing policy tack of the 1980s and 1990s, because it was both temporary and not conducted in an environment of inflation instability.

Table 2.5 categorizes the federal funds rate ratio by decade. Consistent with Figure 2.4, Table 2.5 shows that the federal

Table 2.5. *Federal Funds Rate Ratio*

	Time Period				
	1960–9	1970–9	1980–9	1990–9	1960–2001
Mean	0.69	0.05	0.73	0.57	0.51
t-statistics of Mean Equality (*p*-value in parenthesis)	10.82 (0.00)	9.87 (0.00)	1.95 (0.05)		
Standard Deviation	0.27	0.25	0.35	0.36	0.41
F-statistics of Variance Equality (*p*-value in parenthesis)	1.18 (0.60)	1.99 (0.03)	1.07 (0.82)		

Note: The *t*- and F-tests for mean and variance equality are between the current and successive decades (1960–9 compared to 1970–9, 1970–9 compared to 1980–9, 1980–9 compared to 1990–9). Data are quarterly. The federal funds rate and CPI data are provided by the Federal Reserve Bank of St. Louis (FRED II) and are available at http://research.stlouisfed.org/fred2/.

funds rate ratio was lowest in the 1970s. We also find that it was highest during the 1980s, although the 1960s and 1990s exhibited similar levels. The federal funds rate ratio mean for the 1980s was, for example, 0.73, indicating that it was above the sample average (0.51). The 1960s ratio was also above the sample average (0.69). On the other hand, the 1970s federal funds rate ratio was below the sample average, comprising only 10 percent of the average (0.05).

Table 2.5 also shows that these differences among decades are statistically distinct. Comparing prior and successive decades, we find that the mean level of the federal funds rate ratio of the 1960s was statistically different from that of the 1970s, the 1970s mean level was different from that of the 1980s, and the 1980s mean level was different from that of the 1990s.

We also find that breaking down the data by IOCS (1962:I–1970:I; 1984:III–2000:I) and non-IOCS (1970:II–1984:II) periods reveals statistically distinct patterns in the federal funds rate ratio. Using IOCS/non-IOCS period breakdowns, we find that the mean for 1962:I–1970:I was 0.67, 0.25 for 1970:II–1984:II, and 0.66 for 1984:III–2000:I.

Tests for mean equality (not reported in Table 2.2) indicate that the mean level of the federal funds rate ratio is statistically different between the IOCS and non-IOCS periods, but not between the two IOCS periods.[22] For the two IOCS periods we find no statistical difference.[23]

2.3.2 The Taylor Rule

Using modern macroeconomic techniques, a survey of simulations of econometric models suggests that monetary policy rules should behave in the following way (Bryant et al. 1993; Taylor 1993b):

- The policy rule should respond in a countercyclical manner to changes in both real or nominal GDP (the unemployment rate) and inflation.
- The policy should not try to stabilize the exchange rate, an action that frequently interferes with the domestic goals of inflation and output stability.
- The interest rate, rather than the money supply, should be the key instrument that is adjusted.

---

[22] A difference of means test finds statistically significant differences:

- 1962:I–1970:I compared to 1970:II–1984:II (t-test $= 5.29$; p-value $= 0.00$)
- 1970:II–1984:II compared to 1984:III–2000:I (t-test $= 5.82$; p-value $= 0.00$)

[23] The t-test for 1962:I–1970:I compared to 1984:III–2000:I is 0.21 (p-value $= 0.83$).

With these findings in mind, we use the following Taylor rule[24] (Taylor 1993a):

$$i_t = \pi_t + \alpha_y \left(y_t - y_t^n\right) + \alpha_\pi (\pi_t - \pi^*) + r^*, \qquad (2.1)$$

where the short-term interest rate under policymaker control (i_t) is increased or decreased according to what is happening to both real GDP (y_t) and inflation (π_t).[25]

Consider how the Taylor rule operates when used to institute countercyclical policy:

- If real GDP rises 1 percent above its natural (or potential) rate $\left(y_t^n\right)$, the federal funds rate should be raised, relative to the current inflation rate (π_t), by α_y percentage points.
- If inflation rises by 1 percentage point above its target (π^*) of X percentage points, then the federal funds rate should be raised by α_π percentage points relative to the inflation rate.

[24] In Chapter 4 we highlight various aspects and controversies regarding the Taylor rule.

[25] There is a debate on whether to use forward- or backward-looking policy rules (Meltzer 1987; Orphanides 2002; Svensson 2003a). Forward-looking rules rely on future inflation and output (unemployment) expectations. Backward-looking rules rely on lagged information. Our particular Taylor rule (2.1) is a contemporaneous-information rule (Taylor 1993a). A version of this policy rule is published by member banks of the Federal Reserve System (see http://research.stlouisfed.org/publications/mt/).

- When real GDP is equal to potential GDP and inflation is equal to its target, then the federal funds rate should remain at about a rate consistent with inflation and the real rate of interest (r^*).[26]

The Taylor Principle. To encourage IOCS, just how high should interest rates be raised (lowered) when there are target deviations? Following our argument, we contend that short-term rates (policy instruments) should be altered to raise or lower *real* interest rates. Achieving this outcome requires that nominal interest rates rise or fall on at least a one-to-one basis (the so-called Taylor principle) in response to deviations from inflation targets.[27] Output gap deviations also require countercyclical measures, but the interest rate response should be lower than one-to-one.

The Taylor principle provides added specificity on what it means to act aggressively to stabilize inflation. We argue that policymaker adherence to the Taylor principle ensures that the equilibrium is both unique and learnable (Bullard

---

[26] In the United States, for the period 1960–2000, the real interest rate averaged about 2 percent (see Bomfim 1997; Blinder 1998).

[27] Friedman (1960) rejects price inflation as a target because the link between price changes and monetary changes over short periods is too loose and too imperfectly known to make price stability the guide for a policy rule.

and Mitra 2002). This threshold policymaker response to inflation target deviations makes policy a tool to reduce uncertainty and encourage IOCS (see McCallum 2001b).

Inflation Stabilization, the Taylor Rule, and the Taylor Principle. To illustrate the Taylor rule dynamics (and to see if it coincides with IOCS), we estimate (2.1) by using a rolling regression with a 15-year window. The first data point, represented on the x-axis as 1955–70, is the value for both α_π and α_y. The scale is such that the Taylor principle, *aggressive inflation-stabilizing policy*, is sustained when $\alpha_\pi > 0$.

Figure 2.5 shows that both α_π and α_y deemphasized inflation and output stability in approximately 1968. Prior to 1968, countercyclical policy was practiced on output ($\alpha_y > 0$), but not inflation. Yet, this policy tack still had the effect of raising real interest rates. Aggressive inflation-stabilizing policy occurred only after 1980, when $\alpha_\pi > 0$. For the most part, the Taylor principle was followed between 1980 and 2000 (see Mehra 2002). However, between 1968 and 1980 (the shaded area in Figure 2.5), a procyclical policy of $\alpha_\pi < 0$ and $\alpha_y < 0$ was destined to create an inflation.[28]

---

[28] We also use the Andrews (1993) break point test to determine if there was a structural break in the direction of the Taylor principle.

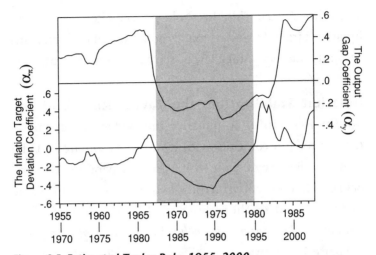

Figure 2.5 *Estimated Taylor Rule, 1955–2000.*
Note: Results for equation (2.1). This is a 15-quarter rolling regression. The real interest rate (r^*) and inflation target (π^*) equal 2. All data are provided by the Federal Reserve Bank of St. Louis (FRED II), and are available at http://research.stlouisfed.org/fred2/.

These findings are consistent with other research, as well as our prior indicator, the federal funds rate ratio, which shows that the Federal Reserve deemphasized inflation stability during the late 1960s and the 1970s. As Hetzel (2000: 3) notes, "Taylor attributes the inflation of the 1960s and '70s

We find a structural break occurs in 1980:IV (sup Wald value = 95.98; p-value < 0.05).

to an inadequate response by the Fed to observed inflation." In other words, inflation instability increased during this period because the Taylor principle was not implemented faithfully.

2.3.3 Taylor Principle Deviations

The Taylor principle is a useful benchmark for whether policy is geared toward inflation stability and coordinating information. According to Taylor (1993a), we define a version of the Taylor principle by specifying parameter values in (2.1) as:

$$i_t^{f*} = \pi_t + 0.5(y_t - y_t^n) + 0.5(\pi_t - 2.0) + 2.0, \qquad (2.2)$$

where (i_t^{f*}) is the predicted response in a short-term interest rate – in this case the federal funds rate – if this version of the Taylor principle is followed. The variables (y_t), (π_t), and (y_t^n) are defined as in (2.1).

Because the Taylor principle is a normative benchmark for an inflation-stabilizing policy, we contrast it with the actual federal funds rate to determine deviations from the Taylor principle. We define deviations from the Taylor principle as the difference between the federal funds rate, which we term (i_t^f), and (2.2):

$$i_t^f - i_t^{f*}. \qquad (2.3)$$

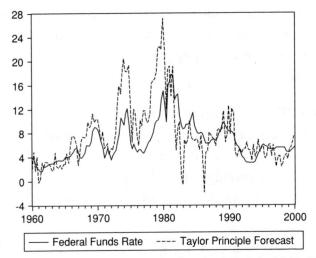

Figure 2.6 *The Federal Funds Rate and Taylor Principle, 1960–2000. Note: Data are quarterly. All data are provided by the Federal Reserve Bank of St. Louis (FRED II), and are available at http://research.stlouisfed.org/fred2/. Taylor principle forecasts are based on parameters in equation (2.2).*

Inflation Stabilization and Taylor Principle Deviations. Figure 2.6 depicts both the federal funds rate and the Taylor principle forecast (based on [2.2]). Figure 2.7 shows the Taylor principle deviations defined in (2.3). Both figures show some important patterns pertaining to inflation stabilization policy. Until 1968, deviations from the Taylor principle were both positive and negative. In fact, the federal

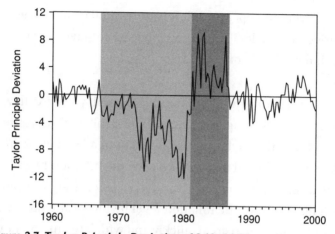

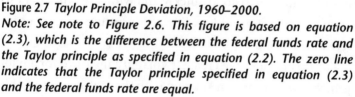

Figure 2.7 *Taylor Principle Deviation, 1960–2000.*
Note: See note to Figure 2.6. This figure is based on equation (2.3), which is the difference between the federal funds rate and the Taylor principle as specified in equation (2.2). The zero line indicates that the Taylor principle specified in equation (2.3) and the federal funds rate are equal.

funds rate appears to have been almost a central tendency. However, between 1968 and 1980, the deviation from the Taylor principle was always negative; the federal funds rate was lower than (lighter shading in Figure 2.7) what the Taylor principle called for in equation (2.2).

Between 1980 and 1987, we see a shift in the opposite direction (darker shading in Figure 2.7). The federal funds rate exceeded the Taylor principle level. From 1988 to 2000 the deviation appears to fit a pattern similar to the 1960–8 period. The federal funds rate appears to have deviated in both directions from the Taylor principle.

Taylor Principle Deviation Volatility. These deviations are interesting, but we can extend this analysis further. Recall that the Taylor principle is akin to a leaning-against-the-wind policy. If policymakers see the inflation rate (output level) deviating from the target level, they are more willing to reduce the inflation level by increasing the (real) interest rate and to do so quickly and with large (basis point) changes. Therefore, this policy action results in greater interest rate volatility.

For this reason, we create a volatility measure for Taylor principle deviations. In keeping with the IOCS measure, this measure is the difference between the standard deviation (21 quarters) of the federal funds rate (i_t^f) and the standard deviation (21 quarters)[29] of (i_t^{f*}):

$$\sigma_{i_t^f} - \sigma_{i_t^{f*}}. \qquad (2.4)$$

Using equation (2.4), we show two cases. If policymakers emphasize inflation stability, then the federal funds rate will

---

[29] See Footnote 2 in this chapter for the formula.

exceed or equal the Taylor principle forecast of the federal funds rate (i.e., $\sigma_{i_t^f} - \sigma_{i_t^{f*}} \geq 0$). The volatility of the federal funds rate will increase. On the other hand, if policymakers deemphasize inflation stability, then the federal funds rate will fall below the Taylor principle forecast of the federal funds rate (i.e., $\sigma_{i_t^f} - \sigma_{i_t^{f*}} < 0$). Interest rates will be less volatile in this situation because they are changed less often and at lower magnitudes.

Inflation Stabilization and Taylor Principle Deviation Volatility. The volatility of Taylor principle deviations (equation [2.4]) is shown in Figure 2.8. As we mentioned earlier in this chapter, the construction of this measure will "push forward" – in time – some of the volatility. Despite this imprecision, we do find important patterns. For example, we find Taylor principle deviation volatility was in a positive direction for all of the 1960s, indicating that policymakers did err on the side of inflation stabilization. The volatility peaked in 1970 and then began to decline to the point where the volatility of the deviations was in a direction inconsistent with inflation stabilization. This "negative" volatility occurred from 1971 to 1979.

Between 1979 and 1980 there was a surge in positive volatility (reflecting a surge in the federal funds rate), but

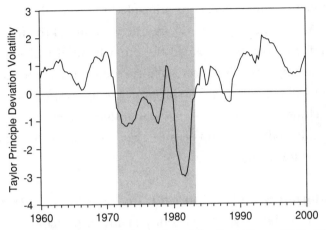

Figure 2.8 *Volatility in Taylor Principle Deviation, 1960–2000 (5-year moving standard deviation).*
Note: See note to Figure 2.7. This figure is based on equation (2.4). Data are 21-quarter (5-year) moving standard deviations for Figure 2.7 (see equation [2.4]). The zero line indicates the average for each series.

this added volatility was followed by a large sign reversal between 1980 and 1983. This period was a time of transition toward inflation stability, and yet the Taylor principle called for even stronger movement in the federal funds rate. Volatility remained positive, reflecting a continued emphasis on inflation stabilization, for nearly all of the 1984–2000 period. The exception was a brief drop in 1988, but here the drop hovered around zero – which means the deviation from the Taylor principle was nearly nonexistent.

2.4 The Interest Rate Volatility and IOCS Trade-Off

Because we contend that IOCS depends on how well policymakers can coordinate the public's inflation expectations, the relevant trade-off is not between inflation and output volatility, but between aggressive inflation-stabilizing policy and inflation and output volatility. Yet, aggressive inflation-stabilizing policy, including the application of the Taylor principle, requires that policymakers change interest rates in relatively large magnitudes (in short order) so that implicit or explicit targets are maintained.

We note that aggressive inflation-stabilizing action creates greater stability in public expectations and means the public will have more confidence and less confusion about the aggressive policy, because they will see the inflation rate stabilized (or reduced) by the changing interest rate. Ironically, however, this greater stability in public expectations[30] – and

[30] As support for this argument, recall from Section 2.1.3 that the volatility of surveyed inflation forecast errors fell during times when the volatility of Taylor principle deviations reflected greater positive volatility (1960s, 1980s, and 1990s).

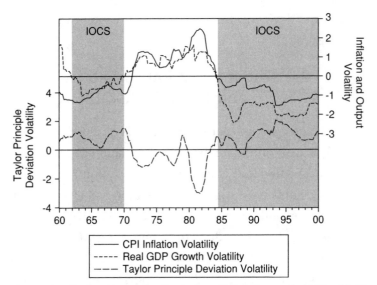

Figure 2.9 *Taylor Principle Deviation Volatility and IOCS, 1960–2000 (5-year moving standard deviation).*
Note: See notes to Figures 2.1 and 2.8.

attaining IOCS – means a greater instability in interest rates.[31]

Figure 2.9 shows that the trade-off between IOCS and interest rate volatility does exist. We combine the IOCS data

[31] We recognize that there will be differences in volatility between short- and long-term interest rates when policy emphasizes inflation stability. The point, however, is that the heterogeneity in short- and long-term interest rate behavior does not preclude the possibility that volatility occurs for both short- and long-term rates.

from Figure 2.1 with the Taylor principle deviation volatility data from Figure 2.8. For the period 1960–2000, note the relation between IOCS periods and periods of greater (positive) volatility in Taylor principle deviations.[32] We return to this trade-off in Part II.

2.5 Summary

This chapter illustrates the macroeconomic stability and instability in the United States from 1960–2000. We find that both inflation and output stability coexisted for a large part of this 41-year period. In particular, IOCS occurred for the periods 1962–9 and 1985–2000, periods that coincide with the longest economic expansions since 1854.

Because IOCS depends on the coordination of price information, we also studied the ability of the public to learn and make correct inflation forecasts. We examined whether the increasing inflation forecast accuracy and volatility coincided with periods of IOCS. Between 1970 and the mid-1980s, we find that inflation forecast errors are the

---

[32] The paired correlation between Taylor principle deviation volatility and inflation volatility is −0.89. The paired correlation between Taylor principle deviation volatility and output volatility is −0.63.

most volatile and that it takes time for the public to learn the equilibrium inflation rate. We note that this inflation uncertainty was also shared by policymakers (Romer and Romer 2002).[33]

In this chapter we have also illustrated how our selected policy indicators, inflation stability and IOCS, are related. We find that when our indicators suggest an inflation-stabilizing policy tack, IOCS exists. This relation is consistent with our argument that policymakers can serve as information co-ordinators when they implement and sustain an inflation-stabilizing policy. Policymakers who emphasize inflation stabilization minimize confusion in inflation forecasts, which can reduce volatility in output and inflation.

Taken altogether, the policy and economic indicators reveal some important patterns. These relations appeared in the mid-1960s, the mid- to late 1970s, and the early 1980s. The changes in the policy indicators preceded and accompanied cyclical patterns in inflation and output volatility and also in the surveyed inflation expectations and inflation forecast errors.

Starting in the mid-1960s, policy indicators showed a gradual movement toward deemphasizing inflation stability.

---

[33] See Footnote 11 on page 48.

The federal funds rate ratio began a nearly continuous decline, and this movement reflected the failure to raise short-term interest rates to stem a gradual surge in inflation. Policymakers tolerated a low nominal (real) interest rate. The Taylor rule showed a similar pattern by exhibiting a procyclical and inflationary policy stance.

By the late 1960s and early 1970s, economic indicators began to reflect greater volatility.[34] Inflation forecasts showed larger mean forecasts, which reflected the gradual and tolerated increases in inflation. During this period the volatility in inflation, output, and inflation forecast errors also started to increase. From the mid- to late 1970s, policy continued to deemphasize inflation stability, and economic indicators became increasingly volatile. Inflation forecasts continued to reflect the increasing level of inflation. Violent cyclical swings in inflation and output volatility and in inflation forecast errors occurred with successively greater severity. For the most part, there was little evidence of a sustained inflation-stabilizing countercyclical policy during much of the 1970s.

However, beginning in the early 1980s, there was a decided change toward an aggressive inflation-stabilizing

[34] See Figures 2.1, 2.2, and 2.3.

policy. This policy shift has been maintained since then. By the mid-1980s, our economic indicators began a precipitous drop in either their mean levels or their overall volatility. IOCS returned to levels consistent with the early to mid-1960s.

It could be argued that the superior business cycle performance is a function of many factors that are not related to inflation-stabilizing policies (see, for example, Bernanke and Mihov 1998a, b; Sims 1998; Stock and Watson 2002, 2003). Undoubtedly, bad luck played some part during the stagflation of the 1970s, and good luck played some part during the economic expansions of the 1980s and 1990s. Unforeseen supply shocks in the 1970s were adverse, and some supply shocks in the 1980s and 1990s were salutary. However, the 1980s and 1990s also experienced their share of adverse shocks in the form of the credit crunch in the late 1980s and the 1998 currency crisis. Therefore, good or bad luck is only a part of the story, and we argue that it is smaller than inflation stabilizing policy.[35]

---

[35] Sustained expansions are also associated with service sector expansion, improved inventory control, and the ongoing technology shock.

We contend that monetary policy has an important effect on business cycle performance.[36] Since the early 1980s, for example, monetary policy actions have been much more reactive to changes in inflation. Furthermore, we assert that more prompt and reactive policy has kept inflation stable and contributed to simultaneous reductions in inflation and output volatility.

As a final point, we find that inflation-stabilizing policy leads to greater volatility in interest rates. Yet, added interest rate volatility creates greater certainty in inflation expectations and consequently is associated with IOCS. Therefore, the traditional trade-off between inflation and output volatility is supplanted by a trade-off between interest rate volatility and IOCS.

---

[36] Stock and Watson (2002) find that improved monetary policy could account for 20 to 30 percent of the volatility reduction and that smaller shocks probably account for most of the rest.

— ✣ CHAPTER THREE ✣ —

Policy Evolution:
1960 to 2000

I f we consider U.S. IOCS performance in the last 40-
plus years and classify this period according to inflation-
stabilizing policy stances, a few facts emerge. Between 1960
and 2000, policy practices that emphasize and deemphasize
inflation stability coincide with distinct IOCS and non-IOCS
behavior. Among the more dramatic business cycle episodes
was the stagflation of the 1970s, the sharp disinflation of the
early 1980s, and the expansions of the 1980s and 1990s.[1]

---

[1] We argue that these episodes signify fundamental structural relations
that are repeated over many different eras. One such relation is the
effect that policy shifts have on interest rates and inflation. Huizinga
and Mishkin (1986) find that in both the 1920s and 1970s, changes in
policy sharply reduced the inflation rate but also led to a significant
rise in ex-post and ex-ante real interest rates (see Sheffrin 1989:
77–79).

To gain a deeper understanding of the relation between policy and IOCS, we discuss these patterns in the context of various historical events (see, for example, Mayer 1999; Taylor 1999a; Orphanides 2003). These events precipitated various policy reactions, which in turn had important economic outcomes. These economic outcomes are associated with the emphasis and deemphasis placed on inflation-stabilizing policy actions (Clarida et al. 2000).

In this chapter we also demonstrate that the variability in policy (and IOCS) was not haphazard, but stemmed from changes in scientific research concerning the Phillips curve. Recall that our view is that academic ideas and policy implementation should be blurred. Indeed, both academic and policymaker attitudes toward the Phillips curve best illustrate whether policymakers are going to act in ways that facilitate information coordination.

Indeed, we do find that policy implementation deemphasized and then reemphasized inflation stability as academic views on the Phillps curve evolved. Our focused historical analysis reflects, in part, the findings of others (see Stein 1994; DeLong 1997; Mayer 1999; Romer and Romer 2002; Nelson 2004), but we also find evidence consistent with changes in our policy indicators: the federal funds rate ratio, Taylor rule, and volatility of deviations from the Taylor principle.[2]

Our historical analysis also shows that transitions to inflation stability were not cheap socially or economically.[3] It is a well-known fact that in the short term, monetary policy actions favored some societal segments and harmed others in direct, palpable ways. Restrictive measures to counter inflation helped those on fixed incomes, but these policies came at the expense of such groups, as builders, labor, and export-dependent industries, which all suffered disproportionately

---

[2] There are numerous historical accounts of macroeconomic policy and outcomes in the aftermath of World War II. These include but are not limited to Melton (1985), Kettl (1986), Volcker and Gyothen (1992), Goodfriend (1993), Havrilesky (1993), Stein (1994), Granato (1996), DeLong (1997), Mayer (1999), Taylor (1999a), Granato, Diller, and Peterson (2002), Sargent (2002), Orphanides (2002, 2003), Meyer (2004), Nelson (2004), and Romer and Romer (2002, 2004). The sources of historical information include interviews, personal recollection, and published economic reports by the various economic policymaking bodies (i.e., Economic Report of the President, Federal Open Market Committee Minutes, Federal Reserve Annual Report).

[3] In Chapter 9, we discuss (briefly) how our model could be augmented to include social and political forces. The purpose of this chapter is to show how policy attitudes toward inflation stabilization evolve and that such attitudes are shaped by factors that this historical account can highlight.

from higher interest rates, a strong dollar, and higher unemployment.

On the other hand, although expansionary monetary policies may benefit some groups, their inflationary effects typically hurt others, such as investors and pensioners. In general, the very nature of monetary policy ensures that, no matter what policy stance is followed, the outcome will have important social, political, and economic ramifications. These consequences influence how policymakers view the overall effectiveness of policy.

3.1 The 1960s: Deemphasizing Inflation Stability

Herbert Stein (1994) notes that the Kennedy administration came to office with the goal of "getting the country moving again." The intention was to make improvements in four related economic areas: unemployment, economic growth, per capita income growth, and poverty. These goals were encouraged in part by the incoming economic advisory team.

The early 1960s were a time when macroeconomic policymakers (advisors) were placing increasing reliance on scientific research. Policy simulations, for example, could be used to explore the macroeconomic effects of various monetary and fiscal initiatives. The "structural" relations that informed these policy simulations were of central importance.

Perhaps no structural relation had more effect on macroeconomic policy than the relation between inflation and unemployment. In 1958, A. W. Phillips showed empirically that there was an inverse relation between nominal wages and unemployment: higher unemployment was associated with lower wages, and higher wages were associated with lower unemployment. This relation was extended to incorporate a trade-off between inflation and unemployment.[4]

In the late 1950s and up to the late 1960s, many economists assumed that there was a stable trade-off between unemployment (output) and inflation. This stable relation could be graphically demonstrated by using what is now called the Phillips curve.[5] This assumption of a stable

[4] Fisher (1926/1973) conducted an earlier statistical investigation of the relation between inflation and the unemployment rate. He concluded his analysis by saying that "the ups and downs of employment are the effects, in large measure, of the rises and falls of prices, due in turn to the inflation and deflation of money and credit" (p. 792).

[5] Samuelson and Solow (1960) wrote a paper associated with the thinking that the Phillips curve was structural.

relation had a powerful appeal to policymakers, who could observe the corresponding rates of inflation and unemployment on the Phillips curve and formulate (with the use of policy simulations) an appropriate stimulative or restrictive monetary and fiscal policy.

Given this scientific backdrop one would expect that Kennedy administration policy would be prone to deemphasizing inflation stability. After all, inflation was hovering around 1 percent during the late 1950s and early 1960s. Combine this fact with the policy bent of Kennedy's advisors, who were very interested in stimulating the economy, and you had the recipe for a new surge in inflation. Still, his advisors, consistent with the findings of Samuelson and Solow (1960), were not about to support policies that would ignite a new inflation. The "economists who came into office with President Kennedy did not overlook the inflation problem. They only thought that they could manage it, like everything else"(Stein 1994: 97).

To further dispel rumors that he was unsympathetic to the goal of inflation stability, Kennedy selected a noted supporter of Federal Reserve autonomy, Robert Roosa, to serve as Treasury Undersecretary for Monetary Affairs (Canterbery 1968; Havrilesky 1993). The move to appoint Roosa showed that Kennedy was willing to strike a sound

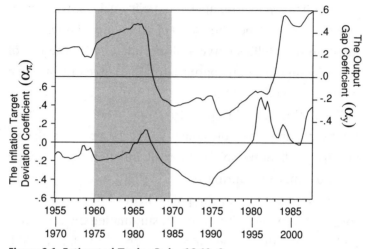

Figure 3.1 *Estimated Taylor Rule, 1960–9.*
Note: See note to Figure 2.5. Shaded area represents period 1960:
I–1969:IV.

balance between the two policy tracks. Expansionary fiscal policies were acceptable, provided they did not encourage an inflationary monetary policy.

Our policy indicators show there was a countercyclical policy in place during the early 1960s. These policies also coincided with the beginning of the first IOCS period in our sample (see Figure 2.1). The Taylor rule indicates that policy was directed toward output stabilization because α_y increased at this time (Figure 3.1).

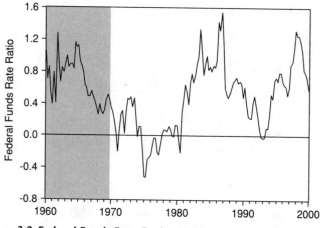

Figure 3.2 *Federal Funds Rate Ratio, 1960–9.*
Note: See note to Figure 2.4. Shaded area represents period 1960:I–1969:IV.

This countercyclical emphasis is also reflected in the federal funds rate ratio. Figure 3.2 indicates that from the end of 1960 to 1962 the ratio rose from nearly 0.64 to 0.99. However, this upward movement was followed by a decline in 1963 to 0.9.

Figure 3.3 also confirms this policy direction. The federal funds rate was raised to higher levels than called for by the Taylor principle. Policy was more aggressive in stabilizing inflation, given the positive volatility in the Taylor principle deviation.

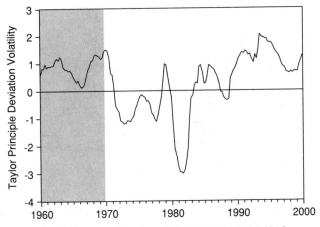

Figure 3.3 *Volatility in Taylor Principle Deviation, 1960–9.*
Note: See note to Figure 2.8. Shaded area represents period 1960:
I–1969:IV.

Monetary policy between 1964 and 1968 was largely determined by fiscal stimulus. Fiscal policy expanded because of a fairly substantial tax cut, the "Great Society," and the escalation in Vietnam War defense spending. These fiscal policies swelled the federal budget deficit from −$1.5 billion dollars in 1965 to −$25 billion dollars by the end of fiscal year 1968. The stimulative implication of these fiscal policies was to place monetary policy in the position of either providing sufficient credit to make sure that the fiscal stimulus was not impaired by higher interest rates or to engage in a nonaccommodative policy and thereby reduce the threat of inflation.[6] For this period, the Taylor principle was followed in a haphazard way.

In contrast to the Kennedy administration, the Johnson administration was associated with policies that deemphasized inflation stability. Figure 3.1 shows that $\alpha_\pi > 0$ only during 1967. Continued emphasis on output stability led to some countercyclical action, with $\alpha_y > 0$ until 1969. In addition, the behavior of the federal funds rate ratio was consistent with Taylor principle erosion. During this period, 1964–8, the ratio reflected the gradual weakening of an aggressive inflation-stabilizing policy stance. From a peak of 0.99 in 1964, the ratio fell to 0.30 by the end of 1968 (Figure 3.2).

In effect, the early 1960s inflation-stabilizing policy stance evolved under the Johnson administration to the point where inflation stabilization was a second-order consideration. Deviation from the Taylor principle was nearly zero by

[6] "Although monetary policymakers were less optimistic about inflation than the Council of Economic Advisers, they nonetheless expected inflation to fall"(Romer and Romer 2002: 22).

1967, down from a prior (positive) peak in 1963 (Figure 3.3). Between 1968 and 1969, there was some increase in volatility and aggressiveness (toward inflation stability) because of a higher real federal funds rate, but it was not sustained. About this time, the intellectual and scientific optimism of the early 1960s was giving way to pessimism. The stability of the Phillips curve trade-off was coming into question. By 1970, policy analysts noted that their conditional forecasts were incorrect. The policy failure was preordained in large part by the failure to reconcile the empirical relations with standard models in economics. In the latter part of the 1960s, Friedman (1968) and Phelps (1968), using both formal and nonformal theoretical arguments, demonstrated that the underlying Phillips curve assumptions were inconsistent with basic economic theory.

In particular, Friedman and Phelps emphasized that the Phillips curve is inaccurate when the public's inflation expectations are taken into consideration. They argued that a stimulative policy could lower unemployment for a brief time if workers' wage demands did not keep up with inflation. Friedman and Phelps reasoned that workers could not be fooled for long and would eventually correct this mistake. However, during this transition to correcting the inflation expectation error, unemployment would fall because wages had not kept pace with inflation.

The scientific consequence is that expectation errors on inflation are important in determining the level of unemployment. Friedman (1968) reiterates this point and then draws its policy implications:

There is always a temporary trade-off between inflation and unemployment; there is no permanent trade-off. The temporary trade-off comes not from anticipated inflation per se, but from unanticipated inflation, which generally means, from a rising rate of inflation.... A rising rate of inflation may reduce unemployment, a high rate will not (p. 11).

With this reasoning, there could be no stable or predictable Phillips curve trade-off.

The policy and social implications were both equally clear. If policymakers, for example, attempted to reduce the existing rate of unemployment below its *natural rate*, the result would be more volatile swings in monetary policy and, by implication, output, prices, and unemployment. Indeed, such policies would eventually be self-defeating, creating a combination of higher unemployment and higher inflation – or what came to be known as stagflation.

3.2 The 1970s: Inflation Instability and Stagflation

Policy issues in the 1970s were framed against the backdrop of stagflation.[7] The predictions of Friedman and Phelps were largely realized: stimulative policies produced both higher unemployment and higher inflation. The stable Phillips curve trade-off was contradicted. "The 1970 Economic Report of the President suggested instead that there was a long-run vertical Phillips curve and that society could have any inflation rate it wanted at the natural rate of unemployment"(Romer and Romer 2002: 24). A disagreement would eventually center on what was the natural rate.

Implicit in the Friedman and Phelps argument was consideration of public inflation expectations and how these expectations would influence labor contracts, interest rates, and the overall effectiveness of stimulative or restrictive policies. By this time, inflation expectations were embedded in public forecasts. Friedman and Schwartz (1970) show that

---

[7] There is a line of argument that supply (i.e., oil price) shocks caused the double-digit inflation of the 1970s because monetary authorities "accommodated" the recessionary effect of the supply shocks (see Blinder 1982). Yet, DeLong (1997) argues that inflation began its upward surge before the supply shocks occurred. We hold the same view as DeLong.

interest rates began to incorporate an inflation premium (i.e., the Fisher Effect). This effect also influenced plans (contracts), which were now being negotiated with the intent of covering expected inflation plus a premium.

With inflation expectations becoming increasingly relevant to public forecasts, efforts to reduce inflation in a timely manner became more difficult politically, requiring far more sustained, restrictive policies. During 1969 and until the summer of 1971, the Nixon administration tried to reduce inflation while only causing minimal increases in unemployment. Despite its failure to reduce inflation expectations, this restrictive monetary policy produced dramatic economic losses. Between 1969 and 1970, the unemployment rate increased from 3.5 percent to almost 6 percent whereas inflation went from 5.5 percent to 5.7 percent. Our data also suggest that this was the end of the first IOCS period (see Figure 2.1).

In response to the failure to reduce inflation expectations and lacking the will to support a sustained, restrictive monetary policy, the Nixon administration imposed wage and price controls. Starting in August 1971 and continuing for a 90-day period, wages and prices were frozen. The price freeze was subsequently followed by additional phases of wage and price controls that were less encompassing in

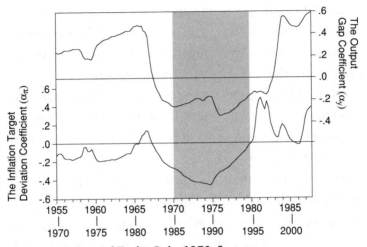

Figure 3.4 *Estimated Taylor Rule, 1970–9.*
Note: See note to Figure 2.5. Shaded area represents period 1970:
I–1979:IV.

scope. Although the price controls did produce a small deceleration of inflation, they did not reduce inflation expectations, because the public believed that prices would rise once the wage and price controls ended. The rate of inflation in 1971 was still greater than it was in 1968 (4.2 percent) and more than four times greater than it was in 1961.

Our policy indicators reveal that monetary policy emphasized the avoidance of a major recession, rather than the reduction of inflation. In Figure 3.4, we find that during this period, the Taylor principle was no longer being followed (α_y and $\alpha_\pi < 0$), suggesting that implementation of an aggressive inflation-stabilizing policy had ceased.

Figure 3.5 shows that the federal funds rate ratio, after initially rising in 1969 to 0.40, began a steady decline, falling to 0.06 in 1971. Figure 3.5 also indicates that the federal funds rate ratio increased the following year. The increase in the ratio was less a function of an increase in the federal funds rate, which was falling over this period, than it was a function of price controls imposed in August 1971.

The volatility in Taylor principle deviations peaked in 1970 in the direction of inflation stabilization (see Figure 3.6). However, the source of this movement, as we can see from Figure 3.4, is not sequential monetary policy efforts. Indeed, this change is the beginning of the abandonment of using aggressive inflation-stabilizing policy.

Erratic behavior defined the period 1972–4. It is clear from Figures 3.4–3.6 that an inflation-stabilizing policy was not a priority. In Figure 3.5, although we can see that the federal funds rate ratio actually increased (0.32 in 1972, peaking at 0.34 in 1973), this rise was due primarily to a steady increase in the federal funds rate, as well as price controls. Absent price controls, the ratio would have been much lower

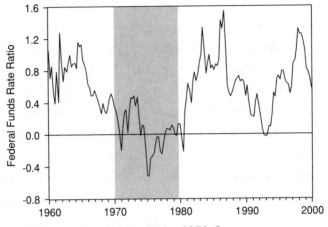

Figure 3.5 *Federal Funds Rate Ratio, 1970–9.*
Note: See note to Figure 2.4. Shaded area represents period 1970: I–1979:IV.

(it fell below zero in 1974 after the controls were lifted). This lack of aggressiveness is confirmed by the behavior illustrated in Figures 3.4 and 3.6.

Our indicators also suggest that inflation stabilization was not maintained between 1974 and 1976. Although inflation did decrease in 1976 from 1974 levels (11 percent to 5.8 percent), the policy did not sustain the disinflation. Figure 3.4 shows that the Taylor rule does not reflect countercyclical movements in either α_y and α_π. Figure 3.5 indicates that the federal funds rate ratio never rose above

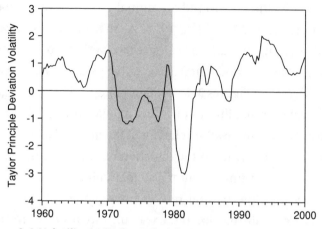

Figure 3.6 *Volatility in Taylor Principle Deviation, 1970–9.*
Note: See note to Figure 2.4. Shaded area represents period 1970:
I–1979:IV.

zero, and Figure 3.6 shows that Taylor principle deviations
were less volatile and in the direction (negative) of inflation
instability.

If erratic behavior characterized policymaker actions toward inflation stability in the early and mid-1970s, the
change in presidential administrations in 1977 signaled a
further shift toward the deemphasis of inflation stability
(Stein 1994). During the Carter administration, various
monetary policy indicators reflected an emphasis on stimulating economic growth. The money supply, as represented

by M1, fluctuated around an annual growth rate of 8 per-cent during 1977 and late 1978. At that time, this growth rate was higher than for comparable periods in the post–World War II period. These stimulative policy initiatives are all reflected in Figures 3.4–3.6. Our policy indicators suggest that inflation stabilization was not a policy priority, because the indicators follow the behavior of the mid-1970s and then take it a step further in the direction of inflation instability.

The Carter administration also maintained the belief and attitude that the natural rate of unemployment was rela-tively low and that inflation was unresponsive to restric-tive policies (Romer and Romer 2002: 61–62). This belief was clearly reflected in the policy choices of this period. As Figures 3.4–3.6 demonstrate, the Taylor rule results (α_π, $\alpha_y < 0$) are consistent with the behavior in the federal funds rate ratio for this decade. Inflation stability was not a prior-ity, because there was no consistent adherence to the Taylor principle. In addition, policy was actually *procyclical* for out-put. The consequences were sustained inflationary bursts and increased inflation volatility.

Between 1976 and 1979, inflation rose from an annual rate of 5.8 percent to 11.3 percent. Inflation expectations were embedded in contracts and were increasing. Average nominal wage growth grew from 6 to 8 percent per year

(Romer and Romer 2002). In October 1979, largely in response to this inflationary surge, the Carter administration and the Federal Reserve embarked on what appeared to be an aggressive inflation-stabilizing policy.[8] During the months after the October 1979 policy shift, the public, now with embedded inflation expectations (Fisher Effect), did not initially alter its inflation forecasts and behavior.

As a result, by the middle of March 1980 the Carter administration instituted credit controls that had an immediate and severe effect on borrowing (see Goodfriend 1995). Policymakers soon realized that economic activity was going to come to a crashing halt.[9] The inflation-stabilizing policy

---

[8] It could be argued that the Carter administration's move toward a disinflationary stance began in August 1979 with the appointment of Paul Volcker as chairman of the Federal Reserve. Yet, the execution of the inflation-stabilizing policy did not begin until October 1979. Under Volcker's chairmanship, between August and October the federal funds rate showed little movement. Thus, despite the Volcker appointment and his supposed inflation-stabilizing stance, the status quo was still in effect prior to the announced policy shift in October 1979.

[9] Greider (1987) notes, "The recession, long predicted by forecasters, finally began in earnest. But it was not the gradual contraction that many had expected. The loss of economic activity was swift and alarmingly steep. Within three months the Gross National Product would shrink by 10 percent – the sharpest recession in thirty-five years. For a time it looked like a free-fall descent" (p. 185).

would be reversed, but at great cost, because policymakers had to repudiate the policy shift. To renege on their initial objective "... would undermine all they were trying to accomplish on price inflation and also destabilize the American economy" (Greider 1987: 197).

3.3 The 1980s: Inflation Stability Reemphasized

The aborted Volcker disinflation and subsequent policy reversal in early 1980 provide one of the most striking examples of the impact of economic beliefs (and social and economic costs) on the conduct of aggressive inflation-stabilizing policy. Furthermore, the effect of the reversal would only serve to solidify inflation expectations at their double-digit levels (see Figure 2.2).

What is clear is that the economic situation at the beginning of the 1980s had been preceded by a period of continued stagflation, with double-digit inflation contributing to such effects as a loss in investor confidence in the dollar and a declining stock market (in real terms). A continued rise in the price of gold signaled, both domestically and internationally, that confidence in the dollar was eroding.

The implications were severe. If public confidence in the dollar was not restored via an inflation-stabilizing policy, long-term investment and stable velocity (money demand) would all cease to exist. More important, a corrective policy would make things worse for real economic factors before it could make them better.

As if these political and economic pressures were not enough, the mix of monetary and fiscal policies placed an added obstacle to sustaining an inflation-stabilizing policy. The monetary restraint, combined with a very expansive fiscal policy (tax cuts and defense spending increases), would increase the government's budget deficit. Consequently, the policy mix had the potential to be self-defeating. Yet, policy proceeded on an aggressive inflation-stabilizing course.[10]

The Taylor rule (Figure 3.7) shows a reemergence of the Taylor principle during this time ($\alpha_\pi > 0$). On the other hand, output stability was becoming less countercyclical (small α_y). Similarly, Figure 3.8 shows that the federal funds

---

[10] Using the 1982 and 1983 Economic Reports of the President, Romer and Romer (2002: 63) also note that unlike under the Carter administration, the "Federal Reserve had the full support of the Reagan Administration in pursuing this policy of disinflation."

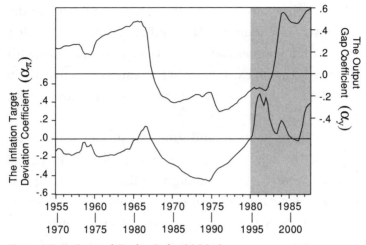

Figure 3.7 *Estimated Taylor Rule, 1980–9.*
*Note: See note to Figure 2.5. Shaded area represents period 1980:
I–1989:IV.*

rate ratio rose from -0.02 in 1980 to 0.46 in 1981 and kept increasing until it reached 1.04 in 1983. The federal funds rate itself remained at double-digit levels until the end of the third quarter of 1982. Figure 3.9 shows that this period marked the start of increasing Taylor principle volatility – erring on the side (positive) of inflation stabilization.

As with all transitions to inflation stability, there were direct short-term policy effects on real variables, such as

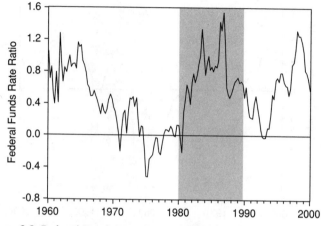

Figure 3.8 *Federal Funds Rate Ratio, 1980–9.*
Note: See note to Figure 2.4. Shaded area represents period 1980:
I–1989:IV.

unemployment. The unemployment rate rose from 7.4 percent in the first quarter of 1981 to nearly 11 percent by the end of the fourth quarter in 1982. On the other hand, inflation was halved by the end of 1982, falling from nearly 13 percent to 6 percent.

However, as economic problems increased, public pressure intensified for a looser monetary policy. In the beginning of 1983, the economy began to show signs of improvement. This economic recovery occurred also near the start

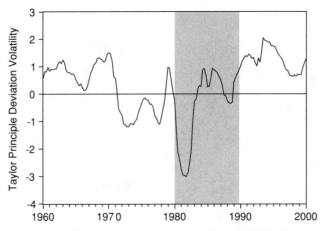

Figure 3.9 *Volatility in Taylor Principle Deviation: 1980–9.*
Note: See note to Figure 2.8. Shaded area represents period 1980:
I–1989:IV.

of the second IOCS period (see Figure 2.1). Inflation was
now between 3 and 4 percent, and long-term interest rates
began to fall, reflecting the decline in inflation expectations.
Policymakers had established and maintained an aggressive
inflation-stabilizing policy stance.

As deficits averaged about 5 percent of GDP and real
interest rates remained high (in relative historical terms;
see Goodfriend 1995), foreign investments flowed in from
abroad. This dynamic helped drive the value of the dollar
up to new, higher levels. The strong dollar pushed the cost

of domestic goods to higher levels. Export-sensitive industries were less able to sell their goods abroad. In response to these sectoral difficulties, money-supply growth expanded at double-digit rates between 1985 and 1986, to bring down the value of the dollar.

Our policy indicators find partial evidence of a weakening in the inflation-stabilizing policy stance during 1986. For example, Figure 3.7 shows $\alpha_\pi < 0$ but $\alpha_y > 0$, whereas the federal funds rate ratio rose to even higher levels, peaking at 1.28 in 1986 (Figure 3.8). The sharp increase in the ratio was more a function of the collapse of crude oil prices in 1986 than of an increase in the federal funds rate. Consistent with these findings, we see that the volatility of Taylor principle deviations became slightly negative (the only time between 1983 and 2000; Figure 3.9). For the remainder of the 1980s all indicators again reflected an aggressive inflation-stabilizing direction.

3.4 The 1990s: Continuity and Preemption

In the early 1990s, the policy of maintaining inflation stability followed the precedent of the 1980s. However, unlike the early 1980s, policy was practiced against a backdrop of nearly a decade of inflation stability, lower inflation expectations, and relatively low interest rates (Mankiw 2001). The second IOCS period was now more than five years old (see Figure 2.1). With inflation stability achieved, the first Bush administration focused its attention more on the federal budget deficit. Monetary policy also saw a shift in implementation, one that aimed at preempting inflations and deflations (Blinder 1998: 17–19).

By mid-1990 there was concern that the budget deficit would accelerate rapidly in the absence of a significant deficit reduction package. Indeed, a series of events, such as the first Persian Gulf War, the ongoing government bailout of failed savings and loan institutions, inflation in government health care programs, and the increased entitlement costs arising from the recession of 1990–1, would push the deficit from −$221.4 billion in 1990 to −$290.4 billion in 1992.

In response to these circumstances, Congress passed a budget package in the fall of 1990. The five-year package contained discretionary spending cuts of $182.4 billion, most coming from defense. Tax increases, including the elevation of the top marginal income tax rate from 28 percent to 31 percent, totaled $146.3 billion during the period. Minor changes in entitlements, primarily to Medicare, farm

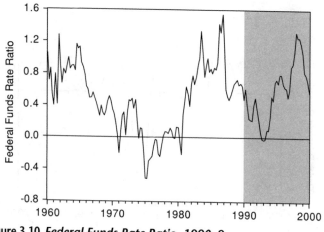

Figure 3.10 *Federal Funds Rate Ratio, 1990–9.*
Note: See note to Figure 2.4. Shaded area represents period 1990:
I–1999:IV.

subsidies, and other government services, added $99 billion. Lower interest payments resulting from the deficit reduction were projected to save $68.4 billion.

During late 1991 and 1992, real economic growth averaged only about 1 percent per year, real per capita income fell, the unemployment rate climbed to 7.4 percent, and business failures rose. Monetary policy, although it did not tolerate a return to inflation, moved in a stimulative direction. Figures 3.10 and 3.11 show a pattern similar to

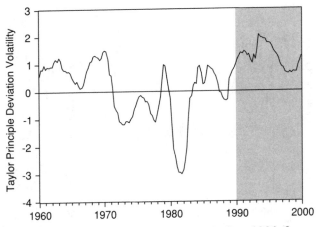

Figure 3.11 *Volatility in Taylor Principle Deviation, 1990–9.*
Note: See note to Figure 2.8. Shaded area represents period 1990: I–1999:IV.

that of the late 1980s.[11] Inflation stabilization was at least a coequal policy goal to the output gap. As a result of the stimulative countercyclical policy, the economy expanded in 1993 and 1994. The improving economy, along with Clinton administration-inspired fiscal adjustments, began to lower the federal deficit, which dropped from −$290 billion in 1992 to −$203 billion in 1994.

[11] Because of the insufficient data length, we cannot do the rolling regression estimates for the Taylor rule.

Another development was the belief that it was important to be more forward-looking in conducting monetary policy (Blinder 1998: 17–19). For example, monetary policy tightened moderately in 1994 and 1997 in response to inflation *threats*. On the other hand, policy was stimulative in 1998 because of the *potential* recessionary effects of financial crises in foreign markets.

The latter half of the 1990s, 1994–1999, continued to show robust economic expansion along with inflation stability. IOCS was also maintained (see Figure 2.1). The federal funds rate ratio began to climb from its low in 1993, reached a high of 1.2 in 1998, and then fell to about 0.5 in 2000 (Figure 3.10). Policymakers followed the Taylor principle and also maintained aggressive countercyclical output policy during this time. Along with sustained IOCS and economic expansion, there were also benefits in fiscal policy. By 1998 a budget surplus of $69 billion dollars occurred. This surplus was followed by surpluses of $124.4 billion and $236.2 billion in 1999 and 2000, respectively.

3.5 Summary

In this chapter we examined briefly the evolution of inflation-stabilizing policy for the period 1960–2000. We found that changes in our policy indicators reflected a mix of economic events and scientific doctrine. These policy shifts created both harmful and beneficial business cycle outcomes. On the harmful side, these policy changes included a reduced emphasis on inflation stability in the mid- to late 1960s and throughout the 1970s that created stagflation and brought an end to IOCS. We contrasted these adverse outcomes with what went right – the reemergence of a policy emphasizing inflation stability – which was associated with the sustained expansions of the 1980s and 1990s and the return of IOCS.

The changes in inflation-stabilization policy did not occur haphazardly. These shifts were responses to events, to changes in scientific doctrine and to the interaction of the two. Indeed, the evolution of economic understanding fundamentally changed what policymakers believed could be accomplished by aggregate demand policy (see, for example, Romer and Romer 2002). In the early 1960s, policymakers adopted the view that there was a permanent trade-off between inflation and unemployment. This view led policymakers to believe that expansionary policy could reduce unemployment with a predictable (i.e., controllable) increase in inflation.

In the late 1960s this scientific viewpoint was challenged by Friedman and Phelps. By the 1970s, policymakers recognized (but did not always implement) the Friedman and Phelps theory. Our analysis also showed that transitions to inflation stability were not cheap socially or economically, and this hardship influenced attitudes toward inflation stabilization and the theory of Friedman and Phelps. It was not until the very early 1980s, when the cost of inflation instability became so severe, that the Friedman and Phelps propositions were followed and implemented faithfully.

Recall that in Chapter 2 we discussed the role of luck and how that could be the dominant reason for IOCS. It is true that luck, in the form of salutary shocks, can influence the economy and confound our ability to determine the effects of policy. However, this brief historical account and our policy indicators move in relation both to the drift toward stagflation (and away from IOCS) and the subsequent reemergence of inflation stability and IOCS.

Although the relation between monetary policy and these macroeconomic outcomes covers a 40-year period and is not part of a structural test, our findings support previous research. The lesson that emerges from our data is that a particular policy stance does matter. Policymakers who ineffectively stabilize inflation risk poor economic performance. To determine the harmful effects, however, requires more than an illustrative statistical and historical examination of the data.

— ✝ **PART II** ✝ —

The Role of Policymakers

CHAPTER FOUR

The Theoretical Model

P art I of this book provided some data, basic statistical analysis, and a focused historical account to highlight the link between inflation-stabilizing policy (related to the Taylor principle) and IOCS. We also showed a trade-off between interest rate volatility and IOCS. Still, the prior analyses are correlations between economic activity and policy instruments. We know these patterns are not the same as specifying a model that can identify causal relations between inflation-stabilizing policy and IOCS.

In this chapter, and for all of Part II, we characterize monetary policy so that we can infer both the policymaker's objectives and strategy. In subsequent chapters, we solve this model in order to demonstrate a behavioral relation that links policy instrument response to changes (variability) in inflation and output. Here, we describe (but do not yet solve) a structural model that shows the aggregate consequences of policymakers who promote information coordination. Following convention, we use a simplified three-equation representation that includes a supply function, an IS function, and a Taylor rule (see Rotemberg and Woodford 1997, 1998; Romer 2000; and McCallum 2001b).

4.1 Price Level Adjustment

The aggregate supply function we use incorporates a natural rate constraint and is a standard lagged expectations, augmented Phillips curve. There are variants of this model that apply to information signaling (Lucas 1972, 1973), institutional rigidities (Gray 1976, 1978; Brunner et al. 1980, 1983), and two-period nominal or real contracts (Fischer 1977; Taylor 1979, 1980; Fuhrer and Moore 1995a, b).

The aggregate supply function can relate policy to information coordination. For instance, Lucas's (1972, 1973) theory of aggregate supply changes emphasizes rational expectations regarding general (i.e., inflation) and relative prices. Lucas assumes that agents are able to observe the current relative price, but that they observe inflation imperfectly and with a delay. When agents observe the price of their own goods rising, they are faced with the problem of deciding whether the price rise represents a change in relative prices in their favor, which would encourage an increase in their output, or merely a rise in inflation. The latter interpretation by agents results in general price increases (inflation) and provides no incentive to increase output.

In Lucas's model, the output and inflation trade-off cannot be systematically exploited by policymakers. Any attempt to generate higher levels of output via consistently stimulative policy will eventually fail. The public simply raises its expectations of what the average inflation level is, from zero or any other constant level to the new, higher level.

However, monetary policy *can* assist in reducing these informational difficulties. In doing so, policy reduces the duration of the effect of these expectational errors on prices. It is the ability of the public to distinguish between general and relative price shocks that determines policy effectiveness.

We can also generalize this relation to alternative aggregate supply functions. All that is required is that the models contain agent expectations. Consider, for example, models associated with a "New Keynesian" perspective (see, for example, Mankiw and Romer 1991). New Keynesian models specify that the short-term inflation-output trade-off exists because of the presence of nominal contracts and imperfectly competitive markets. New Keynesians contend that, because firms and workers set prices or wages in advance of oncoming changes in inflation, the market price is sticky because these agents are unable to adjust their prices or wages in their nominal contracts.

Moreover, some New Keynesians argue that imperfectly competitive markets create a situation in which price-setting firms would not need to adjust their own prices if the cost of adjustment (also known as the menu cost) is relatively large. These price rigidities generate economic fluctuations in the short term. However, in the long term, just as in the Lucas model, the output level is unaffected by policymakers because prices are more flexible.

In these models, the information-coordinating effects of an inflation-stabilizing policy create an incentive for agents to adjust their plans (i.e., contracts, prices) in accordance with the "known" inflation target. This interaction between policymakers and agents is consistent with an IOCS outcome.

With these issues in mind, the supply curve takes the following form:

$$y_t = y_t^n + a_1 \left(\pi_t - E_{t-1}\pi_t \right) + u_{1t}, \qquad a_1 > 0, \qquad (4.1)$$

where y_t is the log of output, y_t^n is the natural rate of output defined as $\alpha + \beta t$, and π_t is price inflation, $E_{t-1}\pi_t$ is expected inflation, and u_{1t} is a (iid) supply shock.[1] We assume that, in predicting future inflation, agents use all available relevant information up to time $t - 1$.

4.2 Aggregate Demand

The demand-function IS curve that we use reinforces the use of agent expectations and also provides an avenue for real interest rates and the application of the Taylor principle. Traditional economic theory maintains that changes in real interest rates affect the public's demand for goods and services by influencing borrowing costs, credit availability, exchange rates, and net worth (household wealth).[2]

We extend this logic to include the interaction of expectations and real interest rates. We use the following IS

---

[1] Following Lucas (1973), we assume the natural rate of output follows a deterministic trend $(\alpha + \beta t)$. This characterization is done for analytic convenience. Our theoretical results do not depend on this assumption. We also consider different properties for the disturbance term (i.e., an autoregressive (AR[1]) process), but again, this characterization does not alter the results we present.

[2] See Bosworth (1989) for an overview of monetary policy transmission mechanism effectiveness.

specification, which is similar to that of McCallum and Nelson (1999):

$$y_t = b_1 - b_2 (i_t - E_t \pi_{t+1}) + b_3 E_t y_{t+1} + u_{2t}, \qquad (4.2)$$

where i_t is the nominal interest rate, $E_t \pi_{t+1}$ is expected inflation one period ahead, $E_t y_{t+1}$ is expected output one period ahead, and u_{2t} is a (iid) demand shock.[3] We assume that, in predicting future inflation and output, agents use all available relevant information up to time t.

4.3 The Policy Rule

Modern research in macroeconomics provides many reasons why monetary policy should be evaluated and conducted as a policy rule – or a contingency plan for policy. Policy rules can be considered both normative and positive. John Taylor (2000b) argues "Policy rules can have normative uses – providing a recommendation of a good way to conduct policy, and positive uses – providing a description of how the central bank actually does set policy" (p. 6). We use policy indicators and policy rules in both senses.

[3] Note that $b_3 = 1$ in a utility-maximizing model.

To capture and evaluate policy effects, a policy rule can stipulate both future and current policy actions. This feature explains why virtually all research on monetary policy in recent years has focused on and used policy rules (see McCallum 1989). Furthermore, policy rules can be reestimated as data become available, and therefore they fit with the idea that policymaking is akin to a dynamic programming problem. As new data become available policymakers can adjust their beliefs about the state of the economy *or* about the scientific doctrine that informs their policy actions. This process includes policymaker beliefs about the slope of the Phillips curve (Sims 1988; Chung 1990; Sargent 1999).

Policy rules state objectives, but they can only be a guideline. They can also show where policy went wrong. We assume that agents understand and incorporate the policy rule and change their behavior in accordance with the expected gains or losses implied by it (Lucas 1976).

Recall from Chapter 2 that we use the Taylor rule because, among other reasons, it is associated with better performance in inflation and output variability.[4] In addition,

---

[4] In Chapter 2, we mentioned that the overall performance of alternative policy rules was assessed in Bryant et al. (1993) and Taylor (1993b). Their research shows that, in terms of output and inflation variability, policy rules that focus on the exchange rate or the

because there are plausible arguments that policymakers follow rules similar to Taylor (1993a) or Clarida et al. (1999, 2000), we can achieve a more powerful description of the policymaker's role (Kozicki 1999).

There is further justification for using an interest rate rule of the Taylor variety.[5] Over the past 100 years there has been

money supply are inferior to policy rules that focus directly on the price level, inflation, and real output (see also Taylor 2001). These authors also find that interest rate rules, such as the Taylor rule, that responded solely either to the inflation level or to real output are inferior to rules that respond to both targets. In our model, we argue for a dual (inflation and output) emphasis, but inflation stability is first among equals.

[5] A criticism of interest rate rules is suggested by Sargent and Wallace (1975) and Sargent (1987: 460–463). The criticism focuses on the countercyclical usage of a (pure) interest rate peg and how this can lead to price level indeterminacy. In particular, a general class of interest rate rules (in a small-scale rational expectations model) cannot be linked to a determinate price level.

However, McCallum (1981) argues that price level indeterminacy disappears – even in the Sargent and Wallace model – if the interest rate rule is endogenized to other variables in the system, such as the price level expectation. Because the Taylor rule is a function of other variables in the system, price level indeterminacy is not a threat.

Along with price level indeterminacy McCallum (1981, 2003) and Bullard and Mitra (2002) stress an alternative indeterminacy – multiple solutions and learnability – in the interest rate rule. We show in Chapters 7 and 8 that adherence to the Taylor principle leads to a unique and learnable equilibrium.

substantial variation in how interest rates have responded to changes in business cycle conditions. For example, since World War II, there has been a larger interest rate response to business cycle changes. On the other hand, business cycle conditions have been the most unstable in periods during which interest rates were least responsive to business cycle changes (Fuhrer and Schuh 1998; but also see Taylor 1999a).

In any event, we argue that a simple Taylor rule is robust as a guideline to policy. We have shown in Chapter 2 that the Taylor rule we use has the following form:

$$i_t = \pi_t + \alpha_y(y_t - y_t^n) + \alpha_\pi(\pi_t - \pi^*) + r^*. \qquad (4.3)$$

4.3.1 Implementation

According to equation (4.3), the coefficients α_y and α_π represent the level that policymakers adjust the nominal interest rate in response to deviations between inflation and output and their respective target/gap levels. Previously, we discussed how equation (4.3) can be categorized as an aggressive (inflation-stabilizing) policy rule only when both α_y and α_π are positive (Taylor 1993a, 1994). Positive values of α_y and α_π indicate a willingness to raise (lower) real interest in response to the positive (negative) output gap $(y_t - y_t^n)$ and when there are deviations from an explicit or implicit target inflation rate $(\pi_t - \pi^*)$. The coefficients typically range between 0 and 2 (Taylor 1999a; Clarida et al. 2000).[6]

4.3.2 The Taylor Rule: Structure and Development

There are several issues of structure and development that deserve exploration (see Blinder 1998; and Bernanke et al. 1999). Substantial discussion of these issues appears in many places (see Taylor 1999b; Svensson 2003a; Woodford 2003), and some of our review involves repetition of familiar material. Here, we summarize briefly some issues that bear on the validity of our policy rule choice. Among these issues are the following:

• the type of policy targets used
• information uncertainty in policy targeting

---

[6] Clarida et al. (2000) refer to (4.3) as a "backward-looking" rule. They estimate α_y, α_π in (4.3) for the United States (1960:1–1996:4). They find that α_y ranges between 0 to 0.39 and α_π ranges between −0.14 to 1.55. They conclude that the U.S. monetary authority moved to focus almost exclusively on stabilizing inflation during this period.

- forecast-based Taylor rules versus backward-looking Taylor rules
- the relation between monetary factors and the Taylor rule
- deflation

Policy Target Choices. Given the relation between interest rates and business cycle conditions, the interaction of research and actual implementation has focused on the use of targets in policy rules. These targets include not only real economic factors, such as output and unemployment, but also inflation and price level targets. These economic factors are precisely what the Taylor rule covers, although the targets may not be explicitly stated by policymakers. The target choices also relate to the ongoing scientific debate about the Phillips curve.

In the United States, there has never been an explicit (numerical), publicly stated inflation target or output gap that the monetary authority was to maintain. There has been legislation, such as the Employment Act of 1946 and the Federal Reserve Act of 1977, that has mandated objectives that the monetary authority should follow regarding growth, employment, and inflation stability, but explicit numerical targets have not been used.[7]

However, other countries have adopted explicit targets. In the late 1980s and during the 1990s, Australia, Canada, New Zealand, Sweden, and the United Kingdom all adopted some form of explicit inflation targeting. These inflation-targeting regimes usually state an inflation target of about 2 percent. There is also a time period during which the governments must respond to the deviation from the target, usually between 18 months and 2 years.

Along with domestic policy rule targets there has been research to augment Taylor rules for open economy targets (Ball 1999; Siklos 1999). Taylor (1993b) shows that policy rules perform better in flexible exchange rate regimes. However, Taylor (2001) also finds that exchange rate effects, *at least for industrialized economies*, are not a big factor in influencing Taylor rules.

One reason for the lack of exchange rate robustness is that the exchange rate affects the price of imported goods

---

[7] Meltzer (2003: 124) notes that in the 1920s there was a focus on various goals and guides for policy action at the Federal Reserve. These guides or goals included, among other things, reserve requirements and price stability. For a comparative country analysis of policy goal evolution, see Siklos (2002).

and therefore the inflation rate. Exchange rates also affect the competitiveness of domestic goods on world markets and hence the level of aggregate demand in the economy. The first effect happens quickly; the second takes longer. The first results in inflation; the second influences output. Under this reasoning, exchange rate effects are masked and subsumed by domestic targets.

However, open economies can be represented by more than modeling exchange rates. Romer (1993), for example, finds a negative economic openness-inflation relation, because economic openness gives policymakers less incentive to adopt an expansionary monetary policy.[8] Romer argues that, in more open economies, policymakers face a larger inflation-output trade-off (i.e., a steeper Phillips curve or aggregate supply [AS] curve). The reason is that, in more open economies, an unanticipated monetary expansion induces a more volatile exchange rate, which in turn generates a larger increase in inflation for a given increase in output. Consequently, because policymakers have less incentive to engage in an expansionary monetary policy tack,

[8] Economic openness can be measured (and therefore defined) as the ratio of imports of goods and services to GDP or GNP (see Romer 1993: 875).

we expect inflation rates to be lower in these more open economies.

The empirical results on the relation between economic openness and inflation (and the slope of the Phillips curve) have been mixed. Romer (1993) and Lane (1997) find that economic openness and inflation have a robust negative relation, but Bleaney (1999, 2001) and Temple (2002) find that this negative relation is not statistically significant.[9]

Still, another way to examine this relation is to use alternative dependent variables. Granato et al. (2006) focus on the relation between economic openness and inflation volatility and persistence. They find that the negative relation between economic openness and inflation volatility and persistence holds.

There is also the issue of price level targeting versus inflation targeting. Friedman (1960) has been critical of either type of target. Although both targets are related, there are distinctions between them. A price level targeting regime can be thought of as one in which the log of the price level has a deterministic trend. On the other hand, an inflation-targeting regime is one in which the log of the price level

---

[9] See Bernanke et al. (1999: 262) for further empirical examination of the relation between nominal exchange rates and inflation.

has a unit root (Svensson 1999). In terms of implementation, price level targeting has been shown to require an immediate response, which could add to business cycle instability.[10]

Information Uncertainty in Targeting. Aggressive stabilization policy requires prompt and accurate assessments of the level of economic activity in relation to the economy's potential. This relation is typically represented as the output gap $(y_t - y_t^n)$.

Mistakes in the measurement of the output gap have been blamed for the policy errors (deemphasizing inflation stability) that contributed to the stagflation of the 1970s. During that period, focusing on inflation alone would have reduced the policy errors (see McCallum 2001b; Orphanides 2002; Romer and Romer 2002; Sargent 2002; Collard and Dellas 2004). Furthermore, unreliable estimates of the output gap can still lead to problems even if the Taylor rule is followed. However, it is unclear whether this issue applies to the Taylor principle. Our results in Part III suggest that the Taylor principle promotes stability.[11]

---

[10] For an alternative viewpoint, see Dittmar et al. (1999).

[11] The same mismeasurement can also apply to price inflation. For example, Alchian and Klein (1973) argue that measures of price

Backward- and Forward-Looking Taylor Rules.

There is a debate about whether policy target information should be based on forecasts (forward-looking rules), contemporaneous information, or past information (backward-looking rules; see Taylor 1999b; Svensson 2003a). In principle, reacting to a forecast is no more forward looking than reacting to current and lagged variables. A Taylor rule that reacts to information in the current quarter is actually reacting to a forecast, because the current quarter information is typically not available until after the quarter. The issue, then, is how long the forecast horizon should be.[12]

Forward-looking rules can have adverse consequences when the models are not considered accurate (Meltzer 1987). There are examples of how forward-looking Taylor rules contribute to suboptimal outcomes (stagflation,

inflation that primarily reflect current goods and services prices are "theoretically inappropriate," because goods and service purchases reflect intertemporal consumption. The suggested solution to this criticism is that price indices should be broadened to include goods and services that reflect intertemporal considerations by the public.

[12] Bullard and Mitra (2002) examine a variety of Taylor rules (backward, forward, and contemporaneous) and find that all these rules can generate determinate and learnable equilibria (see Chapter 8).

deflation). Orphanides (2002) finds that "activist, forward-looking" policy in the United States contributed to the stagflation of the 1970s. At the other extreme, in their investigation of Japan's deflationary episode in the 1990s, Ahearne et al. (2002) find that a forward-looking Taylor rule would have led a policymaker to conduct a counter-cyclical policy that was not aggressive enough to stimulate the economy.[13]

The Relation Between Monetary Factors and the Taylor Rule.

For some time there has been skepticism about the use of interest rate rules. One reason is the widespread agreement that inflation is a monetary phenomenon. If that is the case, then it follows that a money rule of some kind is more appropriate.[14] However, Poole (1970) finds that the volatility of IS and LM curves are important factors in choosing whether to use a money rule or an interest rate rule. Although we believe that consideration of monetary factors, and of money growth in particular, is

[13] A note on empirical robustness. Using several tests for structural stability, Estrella and Fuhrer (2003) find that some forward-looking policy rules are not as stable as some backward-looking policy rules.
[14] See Footnote 4 in this chapter.

important, we also think that money growth measures fail to provide accurate information about overall liquidity effects. Taylor (1999a, b) points out that narrow measures of money growth, such as M1, which should give us an approximation of available liquidity, are unreliable.

There is also the issue of money demand. For years there has been debate about money demand stability. When a monetary aggregate is used as the policy instrument, large unobservable shocks to money demand produce high volatility in interest rates. Monetary indicators also become misleading. For example, Gomme (1998) shows that, in the Canadian episode in monetary targeting during the 1970s and 1980s, a drop in money demand (increase in velocity) meant that M1 was looser than the aggregate was revealing.

The issue, then, is really one of a trade-off between theoretical accuracy and measurement accuracy. McCallum (2001a) finds that excluding money from a model like ours, although it is theoretically an error, is one of sufficiently small magnitude. In addition, a Taylor rule is related to the Quantity Theory of Money (Taylor 1999a), so the theoretical slippage is not as great as might be presumed.

We can illustrate the relation between the Quantity Theory of Money and the Taylor rule in the following way.

For convenience we drop the time subscripts and start with the traditional identity for the Quantity Theory of Money:

$$m + v = p + y, \qquad (4.4)$$

where the variables (money [m], velocity [v], the price level [p], and output [y], respectively) are in log form. Because velocity can be expressed as a function of interest rates (i) and output (y), we substitute $f(i, y)$ for v in (4.4) and note that f is a linear function:

$$m + f(i, y) = p + y. \qquad (4.5)$$

We factorize the interest rate $i = g(m, p, y)$ and note that g is a linear function. To ensure the stationarity of both the price level (p) and output (y), we take the first difference of the price level (π) and subtract the trend of output (y^n) from output ($y - y^n$). We assume that all variables are in a linear relation, and we have the Taylor rule as expressed in (2.1) and (5.3).

Deflation. We have argued that the aggressive implementation of an inflation-stabilizing policy achieves inflation stability. However, the issue of deflation has been raised as a potential problem (see, for example, Federal Reserve

Bank of Kansas City 1999).[15] The concern is that a deflation equilibrium could exist in situations with nominal interest rates so low (near zero) that countercyclical monetary policy would be ineffective in arresting the deflation. For our purposes, we argue that the possibility of an aggressive inflation-stabilizing policy contributing to a liquidity trap or deflation is more of a theoretical curiosity than a practical concern.

On this matter, Taylor (2000a) demonstrates that the Taylor principle makes a deflation an unlikely occurrence and that deflation is not a stable equilibrium outcome (see also Orphanides 2004). Johnson et al. (1999) argue that a small positive inflation target also ensures that policy will be effective in arresting a deflation. Yet another set of theoretical findings by McCallum (2002a, b, 2003) demonstrate that liquidity traps (deflation) involve solutions that are not E-stable or learnable and therefore are inconsistent with stable economic outcomes – and with implementing the Taylor principle.

---

[15] Recall that *deflation* is a drop in the price level. On the other hand, *disinflation* can be defined as an inflation peak that is followed by an inflation trough that has at least a 2-percentage-point differential (Ball 1994).

4.4 Summary

In this chapter and for all of Part II, we characterize monetary policy so that we can infer both the policymaker's objectives and strategy. We devise a simple macroeconomic model that informs the aggregate outcomes that result from aggressive countercyclical policy. The supply function we use incorporates information coordination rigidities. The policy rule influences the information coordination problem by aggressively or nonaggressively stabilizing inflation. Policy stabilizes inflation and output by influencing the real interest rate. In subsequent chapters, our model allows us to devise a behavioral relation that links policy rule responses to changes in inflation and output.

CHAPTER FIVE

Policy and Aggregate Variability

T his chapter solves the theoretical model in Chapter 4
and demonstrates the effects of the Taylor rule (adherence to the Taylor principle) on output and inflation stability.
Our dynamic equilibrium model uses the interaction of policy (transmitted via interest rate movements) with temporary information coordination rigidities. A particular focus
is on trade-offs between inflation and output volatility and
on whether IOCS can exist. We also determine the possible
trade-offs posed by various policy targets (hereafter termed
crossover effects).

We evaluate the model outlined in Chapter 4 by conventional means.[1] As McCallum (2001b) notes, standard

---

[1] We choose conventional evaluation practices so that the IOCS results
are not considered method driven. Indeed, McCallum (2001b) points
out that "this approach has been used for decades, but the tendency

evaluation practice occurs along the following lines:

The researcher specifies a quantitative macroeconomic model that is intended to be structural (invariant to policy changes) and consistent with both theory and data. Then, by stochastic simulation or analytical means, he [the researcher] determines how crucial variables (such as inflation and the output gap) behave on average under various alternative policy rules. Usually, rational expectations (RE) is assumed in both stages. Evaluation of the different outcomes can be accomplished by means of an optimal control exercise, or left to the judgment (i.e., loss function) of the implied policymaker (p. 258).

5.1 Feasibility

In this section we first determine whether policymakers can reach their desired levels (targets) in inflation and output. This step is basic for any further inquiry. We use the equilibrium properties in our model and examine the limiting behavior of α_y and α_π on inflation and output. Recall that from equation (4.3) the coefficients α_y and α_π represent the level that policymakers adjust the nominal interest rate in response to deviations between inflation and output and their respective target/gap levels.

to be more explicit, to show respect for theory and evidence, to utilize RE, and to stress performance under alternative maintained rules is much stronger than in the past" (p. 258).

We explore the following cases:

Definition 1. *Inflation Target Emphasis: From equation* (4.3) *we argue that policymakers have an inflation target emphasis when* α_π *is set infinitely, given a finite and positive* α_y.

Definition 2. *Output Target/Gap Emphasis: From equation* (4.3) *we argue that policymakers have an output target/gap emphasis when* α_y *is set infinitely, given a finite and positive* α_π.

Definition 3. *Mixed Emphasis: From equation* (4.3) *we argue that policymakers have a mixed policy emphasis when they set* α_y *and* α_π *to infinity, given that* $\lim \frac{\alpha_y}{\alpha_\pi} = R$ *exists.*

5.1.1 Equilibrium Inflation and Alternative Target Mixes

First, we consider the equilibrium inflation rate.[2] From (5.21; see Appendix for the mathematical details) we have:

$$\pi_t = \pi^* + \frac{b_1 - b_2 r^* + b_3 \beta}{b_2 \alpha_\pi} + X_t, \qquad (5.1)$$

where $\alpha_\pi > 0$ and $X_t = \frac{-(b_2 \alpha_y + 1)u_{1t} + u_{2t}}{a_1(1 + b_2 \alpha_y) + b_2(1 + \alpha_\pi)}$.

---

[2] McCallum and Nelson (1999) assume $b_3 = 1$.

If there is an inflation target emphasis, we can see that α_π has the expected effect on inflation. Given a finite weight on the output target/gap weight $\alpha_y > 0$, the policymaker can reach the inflation target:

$$\lim_{\alpha_\pi \to \infty} \pi_t = \pi^*. \tag{5.2}$$

This result shows that the policymaker is able to achieve the target inflation rate as α_π approaches infinity.

On the other hand, if there is an output target/gap emphasis, the limiting result with $\alpha_y \to \infty$ (with a finite value of α_π) is less efficient:

$$\lim_{\alpha_y \to \infty} \pi_t = \pi^* + \frac{b_1 - b_2 r^* + b_3\beta}{b_2\alpha_\pi} - \frac{u_{1t}}{a_1}. \tag{5.3}$$

In the mixed emphasis case, we let α_y and α_π approach infinity. We first define the limit value of the ratio of α_y and α_π as:

$$\lim_{\substack{\alpha_y \to \infty \\ \alpha_\pi \to \infty}} \frac{\alpha_y}{\alpha_\pi} = R. \tag{5.4}$$

After some manipulations, the limiting value for inflation is:

$$\lim_{\substack{\alpha_y \to \infty \\ \alpha_\pi \to \infty}} \pi_t = \pi^* + \frac{u_{1t}}{a_1 b_2 R + b_2}. \tag{5.5}$$

The result is that the policymaker is not able to steer the inflation rate to the target level.

To summarize, and in less technical language, we find (perhaps not surprisingly) that the most efficient way for policy makers to attain their inflation target is to influence interest rates in response to an inflation target policy emphasis.

5.1.2 Equilibrium Output and Alternative Target Mixes

In the case of output stabilization we can rewrite (4.1) as:

$$y_t = y_t^n + \frac{a_1 u_{2t} + b_2 (1 + \alpha_\pi) u_{1t}}{a_1 (1 + b_2 \alpha_y) + b_2 (1 + \alpha_\pi)}. \tag{5.6}$$

An inflation target emphasis ($\alpha_\pi \to \infty$) produces inefficiency with the addition of the supply shock, u_{1t}:

$$\lim_{\alpha_\pi \to \infty} y_t = y_t^n + u_{1t}. \tag{5.7}$$

On the other hand, given a positive finite α_π, the same target (i.e., output gap) emphasis ($\alpha_y \to \infty$) produces greater efficiency in achieving the target. In fact, the target can be achieved:

$$\lim_{\alpha_y \to \infty} y_t = y_t^n, \tag{5.8}$$

A mixed target emphasis also produces some inefficiency in achieving the output target/gap. When both α_y and α_π approach infinity, the output level does not approach the natural rate:

$$\lim_{\substack{\alpha_y \to \infty \\ \alpha_\pi \to \infty}} y_t = y_t^n - \frac{u_{1t}}{a_1 b_2 R + b_2}. \tag{5.9}$$

In these mixed target cases it is clear that the limiting policy rule cannot simultaneously steer both inflation and output to their targeted levels. We discuss this possibility in Chapter 6.

In sum, the intuition here is the same as in the equilibrium inflation case above. If policymakers want to stabilize output in the most efficient way, then they should influence interest rates by following an output target/gap target policy emphasis.

5.2 Aggregate Variability

With issues of feasibility established, we now examine the relation between policy and business cycle variability. Recall that our model makes an explicit link between the policy rule (4.3) and equations (4.1) and (4.2). The natural rate constraint of the supply curve (4.1) shifts the relevant business cycle focus to the second moments of inflation and output. Furthermore, because the volatility of the policy rule (including Taylor principle volatility) can also be a concern for policymakers, we also include interest rate volatility (Mishkin 1999).

If we assume that both supply and demand shocks (u_{1t}, u_{2t}) have regular (that is, iid) properties, then we can represent the variation of the expectation difference of inflation as σ_π^2. According to equation (5.22 ; see Appendix) we have:

$$\sigma_\pi^2 = \left[\frac{1 + \alpha_y b_2}{a_1 \left(1 + \alpha_y b_2\right) + b_2 \left(1 + \alpha_\pi\right)} \right]^2 \sigma_{u_1}^2$$

$$+ \left[\frac{1}{a_1 \left(1 + \alpha_y b_2\right) + b_2 \left(1 + \alpha_\pi\right)} \right]^2 \sigma_{u_2}^2. \quad (5.10)$$

The variance of the output level can be derived after some manipulations to equation (4.1) and is reported in the Appendix:

$$\sigma_y^2 = \frac{a_1^2 \left(1 + \alpha_y b_2\right)^2 \sigma_{u_1}^2 + a_1^2 \sigma_{u_2}^2}{\left[a_1 \left(1 + \alpha_y b_2\right) + b_2 \left(1 + \alpha_\pi\right)\right]^2}$$

$$- \frac{2a_1 \left(1 + \alpha_y b_2\right) \sigma_{u_1}^2}{a_1 \left(1 + \alpha_y b_2\right) + b_2 \left(1 + \alpha_\pi\right)} + \sigma_{u_1}^2. \quad (5.11)$$

The interest rate variance follows from (4.3) and (5.25):

$$\sigma_i^2 = \frac{(1 + \alpha_\pi)^2 \sigma_{u_1}^2 + (1 + a_1\alpha_y + \alpha_\pi)^2 \sigma_{u_2}^2}{(a_1 + b_2 + a_1 b_2 \alpha_y + b_2 \alpha_\pi)^2}. \tag{5.12}$$

5.3 The Policy Rule and Inflation Variability

In this section we examine the relation between inflation variability (σ_π^2) and a policy that targets inflation (α_π) or output (α_y). We first show the relation between the policy parameter α_π and inflation variability (σ_π^2) by taking the derivative of equation (5.10):

$$\frac{\partial \sigma_\pi^2}{\partial \alpha_\pi} = -\frac{2b_2 \left[(1 + \alpha_y b_2)^2 \sigma_{u_1}^2 + \sigma_{u_2}^2 \right]}{\left[a_1 (1 + \alpha_y b_2) + b_2 (1 + \alpha_\pi) \right]^3} < 0. \tag{5.13}$$

We illustrate this relation in Figure 5.1. As we expected, Figure 5.1 shows that there is a negative relation: higher values of α_π, which make the interest rate response to inflation target deviations higher (holding α_y fixed), reduce inflation variability (standard deviation).[3]

---

[3] We use the following parameters for Figure 5.1: $\sigma_{u_1}^2 = 1$, $\sigma_{u_2}^2 = 1$, $b_2 = 0.4$, $a_1 = 10.11$, $\alpha_y \in [0.01, 50]$ and $\alpha_\pi \in [0.01, 50]$. Lucas's (1973) estimate of a_1 for the United States is 10.11.

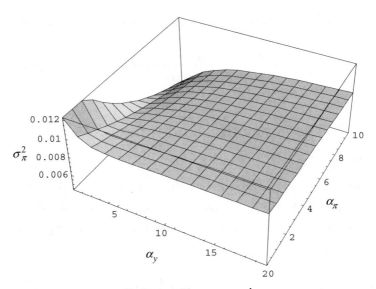

Figure 5.1 *Variance of Inflation Given α_π and α_y.*
Note: See Chapter 5, Footnote 3 for a description of the parameter values used in the simulations.

5.3.1 The Crossover Effect of Output Targeting (CEOT)

We also consider the relation between α_y and σ_π^2. From equation (5.10) we define this relation as the *crossover effect of output targeting (CEOT)*.

Definition 4. *The crossover effect of output targeting (CEOT) is the effect of the change in the output target/gap weight (α_y) on inflation variability (σ_π^2).*

Taking the derivative of equation (5.10), the CEOT is:

$$\frac{\partial \sigma_\pi^2}{\partial \alpha_y} = \frac{2b_2 \left(1 + \alpha_y b_2\right) \sigma_{u_1}^2}{\left[a_1 \left(1 + \alpha_y b_2\right) + b_2 \left(1 + \alpha_\pi\right)\right]^2}$$

$$- \frac{2a_1 b_2 \left[\left(1 + \alpha_y b_2\right)^2 \sigma_{u_1}^2 + \sigma_{u_2}^2\right]}{\left[a_1 \left(1 + \alpha_y b_2\right) + b_2 \left(1 + \alpha_\pi\right)\right]^3} \gtreqless 0. \quad (5.14)$$

Because $b_2 > 0$ in equation (4.2), the first component of equation (5.14) is positive and the second component is negative. The CEOT is ambiguous in this case.

This CEOT tells us that, given the value of α_π, we should be careful in setting the value of α_y (the interest rate response to output target/gap deviations). For a small value of α_y, $\frac{\partial \sigma_\pi^2}{\partial \alpha_y} < 0$ implies that it actually helps further stabilize inflation. However, inflation variability increases as $\alpha_y \to \infty$ (see Figure 5.1). Thus, we know that inflation variability can be minimized by setting the output target/gap weight, α_y, to some optimal value.

5.4 The Policy Rule and Output Variability

In this section we examine the relation between output variability (σ_y^2) and a policy that targets output (α_y) or inflation (α_π). Consider first the relation between the output target/gap weight, α_y, and the output variance (σ_y^2). We take the derivative of equation (5.11):

$$\frac{\partial \sigma_y^2}{\partial \alpha_y} = -\frac{2a_1 b_2^3 (1 + \alpha_\pi)^2 \sigma_{u_1}^2 + 2a_1 b_2 \sigma_{u_2}^2}{\left[a_1 \left(1 + \alpha_y b_2\right) + b_2 \left(1 + \alpha_\pi\right)\right]^3} < 0. \qquad (5.15)$$

There is a negative relation. This result makes intuitive sense, because σ_y^2 is the object of α_y. Higher values of α_y (i.e., making the interest rate response to output target/gap deviations higher) reduce output variability. To demonstrate this relation, we plot the standard deviation of output with both the values of α_y and α_π. The increase in the value of α_y reduces output variability.[4]

5.4.1 The Crossover Effect of Inflation Targeting (CEIT)

We also show the crossover effect of inflation targeting on output variability. We define this relation as:

---

[4] We keep all parameter values the same as in Figure 5.1.

Definition 5. *The crossover effect of inflation targeting (CEIT) is the effect of the change in the inflation target weight (α_π) on output variability (σ_y^2).*

Taking the derivative of equation (5.11), the CEIT is:

$$\frac{\partial \sigma_y^2}{\partial \alpha_\pi} = -\frac{2b_2 \left[a_1^2 \left(1 + \alpha_y b_2\right)^2 \sigma_{u_1}^2 + a_1^2 \sigma_{u_2}^2\right]}{\left[a_1 \left(1 + \alpha_y b_2\right) + b_2 \left(1 + \alpha_\pi\right)\right]^3}$$

$$+ \frac{b_2 \left[2a_1 \left(1 + \alpha_y b_2\right) \sigma_{u_1}^2\right]}{\left[a_1 \left(1 + \alpha_y b_2\right) + b_2 \left(1 + \alpha_\pi\right)\right]^2} \gtreqless 0. \quad (5.16)$$

Like the CEOT, the CEIT is ambiguous, and therefore it requires that we take into account the other policy target weight. Figure 5.2 depicts the CEIT in which, given a value of α_y, the variability of output is decreasing and then increasing as α_π increases.

5.5 Summary

The results in this chapter provide a foundation for the theoretical results in the ensuing chapters. We show that emphasizing output stabilization produces lower variability in output and that emphasizing inflation stabilization produces less inflation variability.

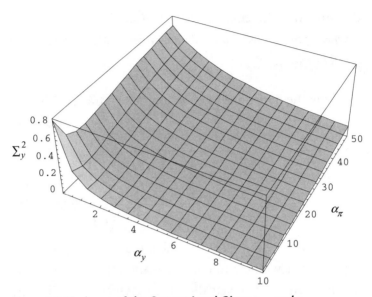

Figure 5.2 *Variance of the Output Level Given α_π and α_y.*
Note: See Chapter 5, Footnote 3 for a description of the parameter values used in the simulations.

Along with these common-sense results are findings that pertain to the feasibility of IOCS. We find, for example, that at some point, an increase in the emphasis of maintaining one policy target (inflation [output]) in the Taylor rule produces instability in the other (output [inflation]). We define this relation as the *crossover effect*. Extending this finding further, we demonstrate that, although a crossover effect and a trade-off between policy outcomes occur (Taylor 1979, 1994), there is also a feasible range in interest rate response in one target that produces *added stability* in the other target. This latter finding is consistent with IOCS.[5]

5.6 Appendix to Chapter 5

5.6.1 Solving the System

In this system we first solve for π_t. We note that $E_t y_{t+1} = y_{t+1}^n$ from (4.1) and $y_{t+1}^n = \alpha + \beta(t+1) = \alpha + \beta t + \beta = y_t^n + \beta$. We combine equations (4.1), (4.2), and (4.3):

$$
\pi_t \left[a_1 \left(1 + b_2 \alpha_y\right) + b_2 \left(1 + \alpha_\pi\right) \right]
$$
$$
= \left(b_1 + b_2 \alpha_\pi \pi_t^* - b_2 r^* + b_3 \beta\right)
$$
$$
+ \left(a_1 + b_2 \alpha_y a_1\right) E_{t-1} \pi_t
$$
$$
+ b_2 E_t \pi_{t+1} + (b_3 - 1) y_t^n
$$
$$
- \left(b_2 \alpha_y + 1\right) u_{1t} + u_{2t}. \tag{5.17}
$$

[5] In other words, although our model stresses an aggressive inflation-stabilizing policy stance, there is support for targeting output stability as well, as long as it receives a less vigorous interest rate response (see Rudebusch and Svensson 1999; Svensson 2003a).

Therefore,

$$\pi_t = J_0 + J_1 E_{t-1}\pi_t + J_2 E_t\pi_{t+1} + J_3 y_t^n + X_t, \qquad (5.18)$$

where:

$$J_0 = \frac{b_1 + b_2\alpha_\pi\pi_t^* - b_2 r^* + b_3\beta}{a_1\left(1 + b_2\alpha_y\right) + b_2\left(1 + \alpha_\pi\right)},$$

$$J_1 = \frac{a_1 + b_2\alpha_y a_1}{a_1\left(1 + b_2\alpha_y\right) + b_2\left(1 + \alpha_\pi\right)},$$

$$J_2 = \frac{b_2}{a_1\left(1 + b_2\alpha_y\right) + b_2\left(1 + \alpha_\pi\right)},$$

$$J_3 = \frac{b_3 - 1}{a_1\left(1 + b_2\alpha_y\right) + b_2\left(1 + \alpha_\pi\right)},$$

and,

$$X_t = \frac{-\left(b_2\alpha_y + 1\right)u_{1t} + u_{2t}}{a_1\left(1 + b_2\alpha_y\right) + b_2\left(1 + \alpha_\pi\right)}. \qquad (5.19)$$

Using the method of undetermined coefficients, we can solve for the minimum state variable solution (MSV; McCallum 1983).[6] Our solution takes the form:

$$\pi_t = A + By_t^n + X_t, \qquad (5.20)$$

[6] See also Chapter 7, Footnote 2.

We solve for A and B:

$$A = \frac{J_0}{1 - J_1 - J_2} + \frac{J_2 J_3 \beta}{(1 - J_1 - J_2)^2},$$

and

$$B = \frac{J_3}{1 - J_1 - J_2}.$$

Equation (5.18) is now:

$$\pi_t = \left[\frac{J_0}{1 - J_1 - J_2} + \frac{J_2 J_3 \beta}{(1 - J_1 - J_2)^2} \right]$$
$$+ \left(\frac{J_3}{1 - J_1 - J_2} \right) y_t^n + X_t. \tag{5.21}$$

The Variance of Inflation. If we assume that both supply and demand shocks (u_{1t}, u_{2t}) have regular properties, we can represent the variance of inflation as $E\left(\pi_t - E_{t-1}\pi_t\right)^2 = E\left(\pi_t - E\pi_t\right)^2 = \sigma_\pi^2$. According to equation (5.21), we have:

$$\sigma_\pi^2 = \left(\frac{1 + \alpha_y b_2}{a_1 \left(1 + \alpha_y b_2\right) + b_2 \left(1 + \alpha_\pi\right)} \right)^2 \sigma_{u_1}^2$$

$$+ \left(\frac{1}{a_1 \left(1 + \alpha_y b_2\right) + b_2 \left(1 + \alpha_\pi\right)} \right)^2 \sigma_{u_2}^2. \tag{5.22}$$

The Variance of Output. To calculate the variance of the output level, we subtract the natural rate of output from both sides of (4.1) and substitute equation (5.19) into (5.18):

$$\sigma_y^2 = \frac{a_1^2 \left(1 + \alpha_y b_2\right)^2 \sigma_{u_1}^2 + a_1^2 \sigma_{u_2}^2}{\left[a_1 \left(1 + \alpha_y b_2\right) + b_2 \left(1 + \alpha_\pi\right)\right]^2}$$
$$- \frac{2a_1 \left(\alpha_y b_2 + 1\right) \sigma_{u_1}^2}{a_1 \left(1 + \alpha_y b_2\right) + b_2 \left(1 + \alpha_\pi\right)} + \sigma_{u_1}^2. \quad (5.23)$$

The Variance of the Interest Rate. The variance of the interest rate is more complicated. We recall that the Taylor rule is:

$$i_t = \pi_t + \alpha_y \left(y_t - y_t^n\right) + \alpha_\pi \left(\pi_t - \pi^*\right) + r^*. \quad (5.24)$$

The variance of the interest rate is:

$$\sigma_i^2 = E \left(i_t - E i_t\right)^2 = E \left[\left(1 + \alpha_y a_1 + \alpha_\pi\right) X_t + \alpha_y u_{1t}\right]^2$$
$$= \frac{\left(1 + \alpha_\pi\right)^2 \sigma_{u_1}^2 + \left(1 + a_1 \alpha_y + \alpha_\pi\right)^2 \sigma_{u_2}^2}{\left(a_1 + b_2 + a_1 b_2 \alpha_y + b_2 \alpha_\pi\right)^2}.$$

$$(5.25)$$

CHAPTER SIX

The Optimal
Policymaker Role

U sing an intertemporal loss function to incorporate policymaker preferences, we build on the findings in Chapter 5 to determine best policy practice. The policymaker's responsibility is to choose a dynamic path for the policy instrument that directs target variables in ways that minimize the loss function. We do not endogenize the loss function to political and social forces. Instead, we use it to reflect the private trade-offs that policymakers face (Dennis 2003).

This loss function (see Rudebusch and Svensson 1999) assumes that policymakers try to stabilize inflation (5.10), output (5.11), and interest rates (5.12):

$$L = \omega\sigma_\pi^2 + \gamma\sigma_y^2 + \lambda\sigma_i^2, \tag{6.1}$$

where ω, γ, and λ are the weights (preferences) that policy-makers assign to inflation variability (σ_π^2), output variability (σ_y^2), and interest rate variability (σ_i^2), respectively.

Although loss functions typically include output and inflation, we also include interest rates (see Woodford 1999). We note that there is disagreement on including interest rates in the loss function (Federal Reserve Bank of Kansas City 2002). However, we argue that including the interest rate term accounts for several factors. One is the consideration of competent policy implementation, which is associated with smooth interest rate behavior (Mishkin 1999). Another issue is accounting for financial market effects, such as an inverted yield curve, asset price bubbles, or general financial stress. Finally, and most important, we believe there is a trade-off between IOCS and interest rate volatility (see Chapter 2).

We assume that policymakers narrow their focus to minimize L for both α_y and α_π:

$$\min_{\alpha_y,\alpha_\pi} L = \omega\sigma_\pi^2 + \gamma\sigma_y^2 + \lambda\sigma_i^2. \tag{6.2}$$

The Optimal Policymaker Role

The first-order conditions[1] for α_y and α_π are, respectively,

$$\alpha_y^* = \left\{ \left[-b_2 \left(1 + \alpha_\pi \right) \sigma_{u_1}^2 + a_1 \sigma_{u_2}^2 \right] \left[-b_2 \omega + a_1 \left(1 + \alpha_\pi \right) \lambda \right] \right.$$
$$- a_1 b_2 \gamma \left[b_2^2 \left(1 + \alpha_\pi \right)^2 \sigma_{u_1}^2 + a_1^2 \sigma_{u_2}^2 \right] \right\}$$
$$\times \left\{ -b_2^3 \left(1 + \alpha_\pi \right) \sigma_{u_1}^2 \omega - a_1^3 \sigma_{u_2}^2 \lambda \right\}^{-1},$$

and,

$$\alpha_\pi^* = \left\{ a_1 \lambda \left(\sigma_{u_1}^2 + \sigma_{u_2}^2 + a_1 \alpha_y \sigma_{u_2}^2 \right) - b_2^3 \alpha_y \sigma_{u_1}^2 \left(\alpha_y \omega - a_1 \gamma \right) \right.$$
$$+ b_2^2 \left(-2 \alpha_y \sigma_{u_1}^2 \omega + a_1 \sigma_{u_1}^2 \gamma \right) - b_2 \left[\sigma_{u_1}^2 \left(\omega - a_1 \alpha_y \lambda \right) \right.$$
$$\left. + \sigma_{u_2}^2 \left(\omega + a_1^2 \gamma \right) \right] \right\} \times \left\{ a_1 \left[-\sigma_{u_2}^2 \beta - \left(1 + b_2 \alpha_y \right) \right. \right.$$
$$\left. \left. \times \sigma_{u_1} \left(\lambda + b_2^2 \gamma \right) \right] \right\}^{-1}.$$

With some algebraic manipulations the optimal values for α_y and α_π in (6.2) are:

$$\alpha_y^* = \frac{b_2 \gamma}{\lambda}, \tag{6.3}$$

and

$$\alpha_\pi^* = \frac{b_2 \omega}{a_1 \lambda} - 1. \tag{6.4}$$

[1] Solving equation (6.2) is similar to Rotemberg and Woodford's (1998) analysis to solve for optimal Taylor type rules.

6.1 Optimal Policy Target Emphasis

The optimal policy target weights have various properties. We consider α_y^* first. This parameter is always positive when $\gamma > 0$. If policymakers put no emphasis on output stability $(\gamma = 0)$, then $\alpha_y^* = 0$. Consequently, any emphasis on output stability makes $\alpha_y^* > 0$.

Now, if we consider the value of α_π^*, we find it can be either positive or negative. When $\alpha_\pi^* = 0$, we know, based on expression (5.1), that the equilibrium inflation rate is indeterminate. We note that when policymaker preferences are such that $\omega > \frac{a_1 \lambda}{b_2}$, then $\alpha_\pi^* > 0$ and policy is aggressive about stabilizing inflation.

In equation (6.4), $\alpha_\pi^* = -1$ if $\omega = 0$, which implies that policymakers are not willing to stabilize inflation volatility. This nonaggressive behavior can be shown from the policy rule (4.3). If $\alpha_\pi^* = -1$, then the policy rule is:

$$i_t = \pi^* + \alpha_y^* \left(y_t - y_t^n \right) + r^*. \tag{6.5}$$

The current inflation rate (π_t) is no longer in the policy rule. Policymakers ignore the variation in the inflation rate and set the nominal interest rate according to output gap deviations, the inflation target, and real interest rate targets. The optimal value of the inflation target rate that stabilizes inflation is $\alpha_\pi^* > 0$, but this value is unattainable when policymakers have no preference for stabilizing inflation variability ($\omega = 0$).

We can also see that both α_y and $\alpha_\pi \to \infty$ if $\lambda \to 0$. The implication is that if policymakers do not emphasize interest rate stability, we can minimize the value of the loss function when $\alpha_y, \alpha_\pi \to \infty$. However, we know from the results in Chapter 5 that a mixed emphasis on inflation and output targets will not reach either of the targeted levels.

Our final issue in discussing policymaker preferences is the potential trade-off between IOCS and stabilizing interest rates. If policymakers care about interest rate stability (an increase in λ), then the values of both α_y^* and α_π^* fall. This result means that policymakers always face a trade-off between choosing a policy that will smooth interest rates or one that will encourage IOCS.

Figure 6.1 displays the volatility of inflation under the optimal policy.[2] We can see that an increase in ω lowers

---

[2] We summarize these results graphically. For Figures 6.1–6.3, the baseline parameters are $\sigma_{u_1}^2 = 1$, $\sigma_{u_2}^2 = 1$, $b_2 = 0.4$, and $a_1 = 10.11$. The policymaker weights for inflation volatility (ω), output volatility (γ), and interest rate volatility (λ) have the values (ω, γ, λ) = ([1, 200], [1, 70], 1).

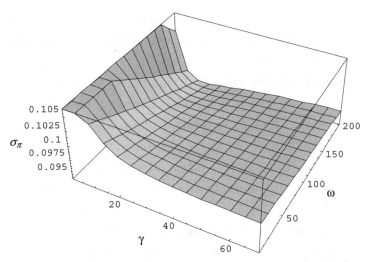

Figure 6.1 *Standard Deviation of Inflation under the Optimal Policy. Note: See Chapter 6, Footnote 2, for a description of the parameter values used in the simulations.*

the volatility of the inflation rate. We also plot the volatility of output under the optimal policy (see Figure 6.2). Using the same parameter ranges for policymaker weights, we can lower the volatility of output $\left(\sigma_y^2\right)$ by increasing γ.

Figure 6.3 shows the interest rate variability under the optimal policy. As expected, we find that when $\omega \to \gamma \to 0$, then $\sigma_i^2 \to 0$. The intuition is that more (less) emphasis

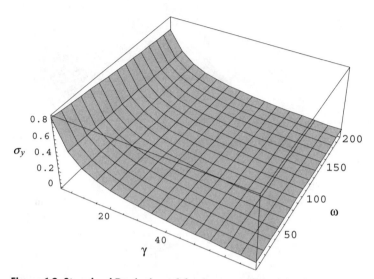

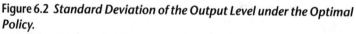

Figure 6.2 *Standard Deviation of the Output Level under the Optimal Policy.*
Note: See Chapter 6, Footnote 2, for a description of the parameter values used in the simulations.

on inflation or output stability means greater (less) inter-est rate volatility. Therefore, there is always a trade-off be-tween an aggressive policy tack geared to achieve inflation stability (and IOCS) and interest rate volatility (see Fuhrer and Moore 1995b).[3]

---

[3] See the Appendix for an empirical test of this trade-off.

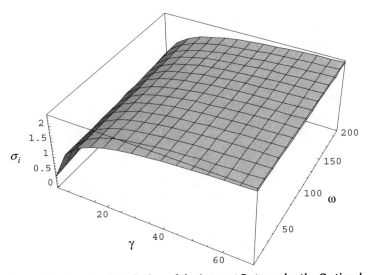

Figure 6.3 *Standard Deviation of the Interest Rate under the Optimal Policy.*
Note: See Chapter 6, Footnote 2, for a description of the parameter values used in the simulations.

The relation between the policy target weights and the supply and demand curves also deserves special mention. Both α_y^* and α_π^* have a positive relation to the demand curve (b_2 in [4.2]). Because b_2 represents the response of output to the real interest rate, small values of b_2 indicate that the real interest rate has little effect on the output level. As a result, the interest rate rule is less effective in stabilizing inflation, output, or both. On the other hand, only the inflation target weight (α_π^*) depends on the supply curve (a_1 in [4.1]). The latter relation shows that high values of a_1 caused by a reduction in σ_π^2 contribute to reduced emphasis on the inflation target.

6.2 Regime and Preference Shifts and IOCS

The convention is to treat policymaker preferences as fixed. However, as Chapter 3 shows, there are pronounced policy shifts caused, in part, by policymaker changes. In addition, we think coefficient drift cannot be explained without the inclusion of regime shifts that are influenced by changes in both policymaker beliefs and preferences (see Sargent 1999).

We account for shifts in preferences brought about by changes in policymakers (Dennis 2003; Romer and Romer 2004). The shift in policymaker preferences indicates a greater or lesser aversion to aggressive policy. If, for example, a change in policymakers results in an increased preference for inflation and output stability, then this change would be associated with IOCS.

We define how policymaker preferences influence IOCS as:

Definition 6. *Inflation-output costabilization (IOCS) occurs when an increase in ω or γ leads to a simultaneous reduction in both inflation and output volatility (as a result of changes in α_y and α_π).*

Consistent with our prior findings on crossover effects, IOCS is feasible only up to a point. Beyond this feasible range of inflation and output target/gap weights (α_π, α_y), an increase in the weight of one variable's parameter in the policy rule will produce instability in the other. In this instance, a trade-off between policy and outcomes occurs.

As with Bryant et al. (1993) and Taylor (1993b), we show that the optimal policymaker role rests in targeting both inflation and output. However, beyond a feasible policy target weight range, the trade-off between inflation and output variability occurs. Figure 6.4 shows the IOCS outcome, given policy target weight ranges.

We note there is a feasible range of ω (the preference for inflation stability) such that both the standard deviations of inflation and output decrease as ω increases. However,

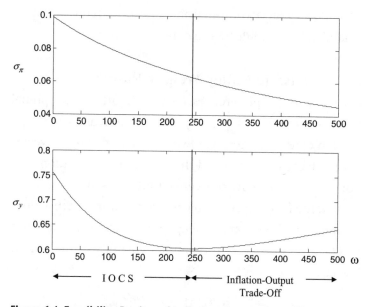

Figure 6.4 *Feasibility Region of Inflation-Output Costabilization. Note: See Chapter 6, Footnote 2, for a description of the parameter values used in the simulations.*

output volatility begins to increase as ω increases beyond the feasible range. This result also holds when we increase γ (the preference for output stability). We find that the volatility of output and inflation decreases, but inflation volatility begins to increase after a minimum is reached. Figure 6.4

also shows that a continual increase in γ reduces output volatility, but with decreasing effect.

6.2.1 Feasible Policy Weight Ranges

IOCS occurs for preferences (ω, γ), the attendant optimal policy target weights $(\alpha_\pi^*, \alpha_y^*)$, and the outcomes $(\sigma_\pi^2, \sigma_y^2)$. We can extend the results to show a feasible policy-weight range. Because we contend that inflation stabilization is to hold relative precedence over output gap stabilization, we present the following example using σ_y^2 and α_π^*. With a modification for the optimal policy target weights in equation (5.11), we can express the optimal volatility of the output level as:

$$
\sigma_y^{*2} = \frac{a_1^2 \left(1 + \alpha_y^* b_2\right)^2 \sigma_{u_1}^2 + a_1^2 \sigma_{u_2}^2}{\left[a_1 \left(1 + \alpha_y^* b_2\right) + b_2 \left(1 + \alpha_\pi^*\right)\right]^2}
$$
$$
- \frac{2a_1 \left(\alpha_y^* b_2 + 1\right) \sigma_{u_1}^2}{a_1 \left(1 + \alpha_y^* b_2\right) + b_2 \left(1 + \alpha_\pi^*\right)} + \sigma_{u_1}^2, \qquad (6.6)
$$

where $\alpha_y^* = \frac{b_2 \gamma}{\lambda}$, and $\alpha_\pi^* = \frac{b_2 \omega}{a_1 \lambda} - 1$.

To determine the IOCS interval of ω, we solve for the first-order condition of σ_y^{*2} for ω:

$$
\frac{\partial \sigma_y^{*2}}{\partial \omega} = \frac{2a_1^2 b_2^2 \left(b_2^2 \sigma_{u_1}^2 \omega \lambda - a_1^2 \sigma_{u_2}^2 \lambda^2 + b_2^4 \sigma_{u_1}^2 \omega \gamma\right)}{\left[a_1^2 \lambda + b_2^2 \left(\omega + a_1^2 \gamma\right)\right]^3}. \qquad (6.7)
$$

The minimum of σ_y^{*2} (given ω) then is:

$$\omega^* = \frac{a_1^2 \sigma_{u_2}^2 \lambda^2}{b_2^2 \sigma_{u_1}^2 \left(\lambda + b_2^2 \gamma\right)} > 0. \qquad (6.8)$$

Expression (6.8) shows that if the policymakers' preference parameter for inflation stabilization (ω) satisfies the inequality $\omega^* > \omega$, then they can reduce both inflation and output volatility by increasing $\omega \to \omega^*$. On the other hand, when $\omega > \omega^*$, the trade-off between inflation and output variability becomes salient. A decrease in inflation volatility raises output volatility.

The relation between ω and ω^* bears further scrutiny. The translation from the preference to the policy target weight is direct. We know that $\alpha_\pi^* > 0$ if $\omega > \frac{a_1 \lambda}{b_2}$. Therefore, the IOCS can occur with $\alpha_\pi^* > 0$ if:

$$\omega^* = \frac{a_1^2 \sigma_{u_2}^2 \lambda^2}{b_2^2 \sigma_{u_1}^2 \left(\lambda + b_2^2 \gamma\right)} > \frac{a_1 \lambda}{b_2}. \qquad (6.9)$$

However, it is also clear that ω^* and α_π^* depend on the preference for output stabilization (γ). After some adjustments to (6.9), we have:

$$\frac{a_1 \sigma_{u_2}^2 - b_2 \sigma_{u_1}^2}{b_2^3 \sigma_{u_1}^2} > \frac{\gamma}{\lambda}, \quad \text{for } \gamma, \lambda > 0. \qquad (6.10)$$

Consequently, if the condition in equation (6.10) is satisfied, an increase in a positive α_π^* reduces both inflation and output volatility.

Proposition 7. *If the condition established in equation* (6.10) *is satisfied, then an increase in ω can attain IOCS.*

Intuitively, the existence of IOCS depends on the demand-supply-shock volatility ratio $\left(\frac{\sigma_{u_2}^2}{\sigma_{u_1}^2}\right)$ and the output-stabilization preference ratio $\left(\frac{\gamma}{\lambda}\right)$. If the demand-supply-shock volatility ratio is large enough relative to the output-stabilization preference ratio presented in equation (6.10), then a policymaker with a greater inflation stabilization preference (higher ω) will reduce (successfully) both the inflation and output volatility level.

We summarize the results of our findings in Table 6.1. We find that, as policymakers' preference for reducing inflation volatility increases (i.e., ω increases), this change raises the optimal value of α_π^*, which reduces the standard deviation of inflation. We also find, consistent with IOCS, that the standard deviation of output falls up to a point. Note also that the standard deviation of the interest rate increases (for the most part), reflecting its trade-off with the other two variables. Alternatively, when the policymakers' preference for

Table 6.1. *Standard Deviations of Inflation, Output, and Interest Rates with Different Values of the Optimal Parameters in the Taylor Rule*

α_π^*	$\alpha_y^* = 0.0$	$\alpha_y^* = 0.5$	$\alpha_y^* = 5.0$	$\alpha_y^* = 50$
0.5	0.0416	0.0384	0.0314	0.0300
	0.9824	0.8211	0.3313	0.0475
	0.0625	0.4489	1.6717	2.3810
5.0	0.0395	0.0368	0.0308	0.0299
	0.9352	0.7881	0.3263	0.0475
	0.2374	0.5530	1.6872	2.3813
50	0.0263	0.0288	0.0262	0.0291
	0.7273	0.6470	0.3245	0.0542
	1.3422	1.4028	1.8568	2.3853

Note: See Chapter 6, Footnote 2 for a description of the parameter values used in the simulations. The table should be read in the following way. At the upper left-hand corner of the table we see that the combination of optimal parameters – $(\alpha_\pi^*, \alpha_y^*) = (0.5, 0.0)$ – results in standard deviations of inflation, output, and interest rates of (0.0416, 0.9824, 0.0625), respectively.

stabilizing output increases (i.e., γ increases), the optimal value of α_y^* increases. The result is that the standard deviation of output falls. We also find that the standard deviation of inflation is reduced for a considerable range of values for α_y^*. On the other hand, interest rate volatility has a positive relation with α_y^*.

6.3 IOCS in the Presence of Exogenous Shocks

There is little doubt that successful policy requires an understanding of the nature of the shocks hitting the economy (see, for example, Ball and Mankiw 1995). Countercyclical policy is best suited to dealing with large, persistent aggregate demand shocks. In contrast, aggregate supply shocks and financial market shocks pose more difficult problems for policymakers (Federal Reserve Bank of Kansas City 2002).

To address this issue we examine the effect of demand and supply shocks on the feasibility of IOCS. Equation (6.9) indicates the feasible interval of IOCS for an optimal value of α_π^* to reduce output volatility. This interval depends on the exogenous shocks from demand and supply $\left(\sigma_{u_1}^2, \sigma_{u_2}^2\right)$. If a current business cycle is primarily a function of a demand shock and the variance of the demand shock $\left(\sigma_{u_2}^2\right)$ is large, then this economic environment means ω^* will also be large. Consequently, policymakers have more room to reduce inflation and output volatility by increasing α_π^*.

However, if a supply shock $\left(\sigma_{u_1}^2\right)$ is driving the current business cycle and the supply shock variance is large, then this economic environment lowers the value of ω^*.

The feasible range for IOCS is smaller, and if policymakers stabilize either inflation or output variability more aggressively, the inflation-output variability trade-off is more likely to occur.

6.4 Summary

In this chapter we extend the model to consider the optimal policymaker stance. Consistent with our findings in Chapter 3, policymakers face crossover effects when choosing a particular policy target to emphasize. We also find that the magnitude of the policy (interest rate) response to the deviations in these targets has a relation to the efficiency of the outcomes for either output or inflation (Clarida et al. 1999, 2000; Taylor 1999a). What matters is the aggressive application of countercyclical (particularly inflation-stabilizing) policy that, when applied within a feasible range of interest rate responses, can lead to IOCS. However, policymakers must be careful, because an aggressive policy tack creates greater volatility in interest rates and is generally inconsistent with a policy that emphasizes smooth movements in interest rates. In keeping with our findings in Chapter 2, we find that the more enduring trade-off is not between inflation and output stability, but rather between IOCS and interest rate stability (see Appendix).

We also extend the policymaker role to situations in which the size of the supply or demand shock variations changes. If the business cycle fluctuation occurs in response to a demand shock, which implies that the variance of the demand shock is large, policymakers have a greater range of feasible policy responses to use to stabilize both inflation and output volatility. On the other hand, if the business cycle fluctuation is caused largely by a supply shock, meaning that the variance of the supply shock is large, the range of feasible policy responses is smaller, and the inflation-output variability trade-off is more likely to occur if policymakers stabilize either inflation or output variability more aggressively.

6.5 Appendix to Chapter 6

6.5.1 The Interest Rate Volatility and IOCS Trade-Off: A Test

The results in Section 6.1 provide a theoretical basis for the interest rate volatility and IOCS trade-off. Recall that we argue that the more enduring trade-off is between interest rate volatility and IOCS, as opposed to the traditionally asserted trade-off between inflation and output volatility (see Figure 2.9).

Here, we use a vector autogression (VAR) to test whether there is a negative relation between Taylor principle deviation volatility and inflation and output volatility. The data are the same as those used in Chapter 2 – 21-quarter moving standard deviations. The unrestricted VAR we use contains four lags of each variable.[4] Because these data are in levels and one of the series is I(1),[5] we rely on innovation accounting only.[6]

---

[4] The Sims modified likelihood ratio test statistic indicates that the optimal lag specification is four lags.

[5] The results of our augmented Dickey-Fuller test show that Taylor principle deviation volatility has a p-value of 0.03, indicating that it is stationary. Both inflation and output volatility have augmented Dickey-Fuller test p-values of 0.07 and 0.65, respectively, indicating that inflation volatility is stationary and output volatility is integrated.

[6] It is well known that a VAR in levels, when part or all of the data are nonstationary, gives distribution results that are nonnormal. This behavior confounds Granger causality tests because they rely on standard distribution theory (i.e., F-distribution).

However, because nonstationary regressors converge at such high rates of speed, the impulse responses will converge to the "true" impulse responses in the limit. Although the impulse responses do converge to their true values, Phillips (1998) finds that nonstationarity still causes some inefficiency (because of the persistence of the shocks).

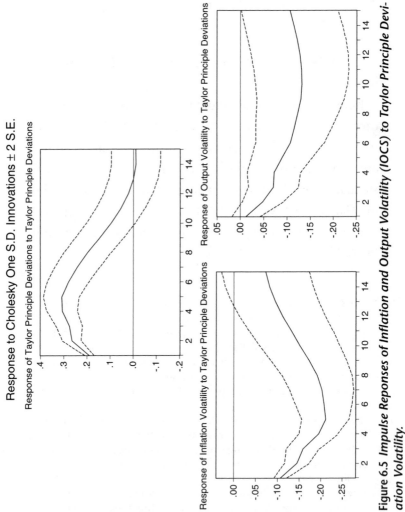

Figure 6.5 *Impulse Reponses of Inflation and Output Volatility (IOCS) to Taylor Principle Deviation Volatility.*

Figure 6.5 shows the results from an orthogonalized 1 standard deviation shock in the Taylor principle deviation volatility.[7] Both inflation and output stability are influenced significantly, reflecting a negative relation with the Taylor principle deviation.

The results indicate that inflation volatility responds first to the shock, with the effect peaking at five quarters, and that output responds later, at about three quarters, with the peak effect occurring at about ten quarters. Although the responses are somewhat different, the magnitudes of the effects are similar (−0.2 for inflation volatility and −0.15 for output volatility).

Another issue is how the Taylor principle deviation shock influences itself. As with inflation volatility, the effect is immediate. It peaks in 5 quarters (0.30) and persists for 12 quarters.

A final issue is the sequence of the effect. Initially, Taylor principle deviation volatility shocks affect both itself and inflation volatility, but the shocks eventually influence output.

---

[7] Recall from Chapter 2 that the correlations between Taylor principle deviation volatility and inflation volatility and output volatility are −0.89 and −0.63, respectively.

This result is only one test, but it does suggest that the co-ordinating effect of policy is consistent with this sequence. Policy changes are made, they influence public inflation expectations, and this relation translates to plans that affect output.

— ✦ PART III ✦ —

Coordination Dynamics

— ✢ CHAPTER SEVEN ✢ —

Coordinating Inflation Forecasts

In Part II, our focus was on developing a small-scale macroeconomic model that captured policy effects. We focused particular attention on how a policy emphasis on stabilizing inflation (adherence to the Taylor principle) could, under certain conditions, attain IOCS. The macroeconomic results presume coordination dynamics of a particular kind between policymakers and the public. These coordination dynamics between policymakers and the public center on the stream of information transmitted by price and on how policymakers could reduce the public's uncertainty about future inflation.

The threat posed by inflation is the noise it brings to bear on the price signals that the public uses when making forecasts and plans (see Friedman 1963, 1977). We know the noise exists, because there is a (positive) theoretical and empirical relation between inflation variability and the mean of inflation (see Vining and Elwertowski 1976; Parks 1978; Cukierman and Wachtel 1979; Taylor 1981). As we have argued, a policymaker's role is to assist in coordinating the public's information by reducing the noise in price signals. We now turn our attention to how aggressive inflation-stabilizing policy (adherence to the Taylor principle) coordinates accurate inflation forecasts.

Policymakers coordinate price information for the public in the following way. When policymakers achieve and maintain inflation stability, the public can substitute what it thinks is an implicit or explicit inflation target (set by the policymaker) for past inflation. In this environment, plans (i.e., contracts) now exhibit (price) stability. In addition, because these plans have an effect on the overall inflation rate, the stability that plans and contracts now exhibit translates into inflation stability and output (by equation [4.1]) growth at its natural rate.

On the other hand, a nonaggressive inflation-stabilizing policy implies that interest rates will not respond to inflation shocks and that, sometimes perversely, interest rates may decrease, providing a procyclical response to an inflation shock. In this case, because of the price rigidities in the economy (i.e., contracts in the aggregate supply function), the inflation shock will not die out soon. The public fails to determine an implicit or explicit inflation target and must rely on past inflation to make its inflation forecasts. There is also the possibility that if policymakers continue to tolerate inflation instability, then inflation persistence will become more pronounced and could take on an additive (i.e., unit root), explosive nature. Further, and perhaps most important, it is possible to infer from inflation persistence both policymaker reputation and policymaker credibility.[1]

Empirically, we should then see drift in estimated coefficients because that is evidence of the changing persistence and volatility of inflation (Sargent 2002). We know, for example, that between the 1950s and 1980s inflation went from a low-order autoregressive process to a

---

[1] Siklos (2002) argues that if the monetary authority allows inflation to persist (i.e., the lagged endogenous term in the AR(1) regression approaches unity), then,

The accumulated record of the past will weigh more heavily in determining inflation performance than a change in monetary regimes or some other institutional factor. By contrast, if inflation persistence falls without a change in policy goals, because inflation expectations are better anchored, then this can largely be attributed to the reputation of the central bank. Therefore, a change in inflation persistence, accompanied by a change in policy goals, may be attributed to the credibility of the central bank at delivering presumably a better inflation outcome under a new framework (pp. 40–41).

near-integrated process (McCallum 1994). It is an empirical question whether policy can systematically alter inflation forecasts and inflation persistence and volatility. Statistical estimates by Taylor (1993a), Clarida et al. (2000), and Cogley and Sargent (2001, 2002) on monetary policy rules (over various subperiods) illuminate possible differences between the Volcker-Greenspan terms and other periods. They find evidence for a systematic change of monetary policy across the various eras.

The challenge, then, is to sort out the competing evidence on whether, as we argue, aggressive inflation-stabilizing policy reduced inflation persistence and volatility and led to IOCS or whether IOCS was a matter of salutary exogenous economic shocks. On the latter alternative, Sims (1998) and Bernanke and Mihov (1998a, b) are among the researchers who present evidence that the data in the United States show that it was not aggressive inflation-stabilizing policy, but the exogenous reduction in the volatility of various shocks.

Consequently, one of our purposes in this part in the book is to follow up on our theoretical findings and evaluations and examine whether it was policy or luck that encouraged IOCS outcomes. One possible way to resolve this disagreement centers on examining inflation persistence.

Our model isolates the effect of policy on inflation persistence and in doing so allows for a distinction between the effects of policy and of salutary exogenous shocks.

7.1 Empirical Implications of the Theoretical Model

In this chapter we merge formal analysis directly with empirical tests and actual data. In the same spirit as Friedman (1957) and Lucas (1973), we show that specific empirical coefficients will fluctuate based on various changes in variables (parameters) in the theoretical model. The empirical implications of our theoretical model (EITM) show the relation between inflation-stabilizing policy and inflation persistence and volatility.

Along with the focus on inflation persistence and volatility we use stability analysis. We use a model consistent with Chapter 5, one that contains a natural rate constraint and in which the interaction between policymakers and agents creates learning dynamics that can result in changes in inflation persistence and volatility. We also extend the model in Chapter 5 to include greater specificity about labor markets because doing so helps determine whether there is a coordination effect that extends from policymakers to the public.

McCallum (2002a, b, 2003), among others, focuses on using inflation forecasts for policy to determine indeterminacies that are inconsistent with learning. The message from our analysis is that indeterminacies are inconsistent with the policymaker's ability to steer the public's inflation forecast to the correct value. We make use of the formal results that rely on traditional minimum state variable (MSV) solutions. MSV solutions are consistent with learning (Evans and Honkapohja 2001).[2]

---

[2] McCallum (2001a) discusses the MSV concept at length, interpreting it as a unique solution that includes no bubble or sunspot components. McCallum proposes a solution procedure that generates a unique solution in a very wide class of linear RE models.

Further details on sunspot and bubble solutions and how they are different from a fundamental solution can be found in Evans and Honkapohja (2001: 178). They point out that McCallum (1983) has recommended use of the term "bubble solution" in reference to autoregressive-moving average (ARMA) solutions (whether or not they depend on sunspot variables).

The terms "bubble" and "fundamental" solutions are both frequently used for the MSV solution procedure. The argument for differentiating between bubble solutions and fundamental solutions centers on agents' beliefs that certain variables matter, even though rational agents could also believe that these variables do not affect the solution. Thus, the self-fulfilling prophecy aspect of the solution works for the bubble solutions, but is irrelevant for fundamental

We also show that policymakers can steer agents to make more accurate inflation forecasts, because policymaker behavior can provide greater certainty about future inflation rates. In addition, changes in inflation persistence (and volatility) play an important part as an indicator for changes in policy. These empirical estimates are also linked to our historical analysis in Chapter 3 so that beliefs and policy actions supplement each other.[3]

---

solutions. McCallum argues that in practice we should pick the fundamental MSV solution unless we are specifically interested in the bubble issue (see also McCallum 1999).

[3] Although we focus on domestic policy concerns and targets (inflation and output), another line of research focuses on how policymakers use exchange rate regimes and targets to reduce inflation persistence and volatility. The results of this research indicate that inflation has more persistence under floating exchange rates than under fixed rates (Alogoskoufis and Smith 1991; Alogoskoufis 1992; Obstfeld 1995; Burdekin and Siklos 1999; Siklos 1999).

Consistent with our discussion in Chapter 4, the effect of exchange rates and exchange rate regimes has also been called into question. Bleaney (1999, 2001) finds that changes in inflation persistence have nothing to do with the exchange rate regime. Using OECD data for the period 1954–96 and allowing for mean shifts in the inflation rate, he finds inflation persistence is similar, across countries, regardless of the exchange rate regime. Bleaney concludes that the reduction of inflation persistence comes from the change of the monetary targets across countries.

In contrast, Siklos (1999), for example, examines inflation targets and compares them to the exchange rate regime. He chooses ten

7.2 The Relative-Real-Wage Contract Specification

To link the coordination effects of policy, we rely on a relative-real-wage contract model in combination with a Taylor interest rate rule (Taylor, 1993a, 1994, 1999a, b; Fuhrer 1995; Fuhrer and Moore 1995a, b). Labor market inflation expectations have been studied in relation to whether poor forecasts affect the natural rate of unemployment (Akerlof et al. 1996; Groshen and Schweitzer 1996). More recently, there has been an emphasis on the coordination of labor market inflation forecasts and inflation persistence and dynamics (Driscoll and Holden 2003; Driscoll and Ito 2003; Rudd and Whelan 2003).

Our model contains the feature of inflation persistence, because agents not only consider a forward-looking component of the inflation rate but are also concerned with the past values of inflation. We investigate inflation persistence because a number of studies argue that models without

OECD countries (for the period covering the late 1950s until the late 1990s): Australia, Canada, Finland, New Zealand, Spain, Sweden, United Kingdom, United States, Germany, and Switzerland. He categorizes the first seven countries as the inflation-targeting countries and finds that the adoption of an inflation-targeting policy is not sufficient to reduce the persistence of inflation.

inflation inertia (i.e., persistence) are flawed (see Siklos 1999; Woodford 1999). For example, Woodford (1999: 13) argues that "the complete absence of inertial terms in the structural equations is not entirely realistic." Empirically, we know inflation in the United States does persist (see Owyang 2001).

The model assumes a two-period contract. For simplicity, prices reflect a unitary markup over wages. We express the price at time t, (p_t), as the average of the current (x_t) and the lagged (x_{t-1}) contract wage:

$$p_t = \frac{1}{2}(x_t + x_{t-1}), \qquad (7.1)$$

where p_t is the logged price level and x_t is the logged wage level at period t.

In addition, agents are concerned with their real wages over the lifetime of the contract:

$$x_t - p_t = \frac{1}{2}[x_{t-1} - p_{t-1} + E_t(x_{t+1} - p_{t+1})] + a_2 z_t, \qquad (7.2)$$

where $z_t = (y_t - y_t^n)$ is the excess demand for labor at time t and $E_t(x_{t+1} - p_{t+1})$ is the expected future real wage level.

We define the inflation rate (π_t) as the difference between the current and lagged price level, ($p_t - p_{t-1}$). Using this definition, we substitute equation (7.2) into equation (7.1) and obtain:

$$\pi_t = \frac{1}{2}\left(\pi_{t-1} + E_t\pi_{t+1}\right) + a_2 z_t + u_{3t}, \qquad (7.3)$$

where $E_t\pi_{t+1}$ is the expected inflation rate over the next period and $u_{3t} \sim iid\left(0, \sigma_{u_3}^2\right).$[4]

Equation (7.3) captures the main characteristic of inflation persistence. Because agents make plans about their real wages based on both the past and future periods, they take into consideration the lagged price level (p_{t-1}) as they adjust (negotiate) their real wage at time t. This model feature allows the inflation rate to depend on both the expected inflation rate and the past inflation level.

7.2.1 The IS Specification

For ease of calculation (and without loss of generality), we simplify the IS curve presented in (4.2).[5] Equation (7.4) represents a standard IS curve where the quantity demanded on

---

[4] The output term in equation (7.3) actually is a moving average of the current and the lagged output gap, $\frac{\gamma}{2}(z_t + z_{t-1})$. However, Fuhrer (1995) assumes the output term is the current output gap, γz_t, for simplicity.

[5] We use a more general model in Chapter 8 to demonstrate the robustness (i.e., no indeterminacies) of an aggressive inflation-stabilizing policy.

output relative to natural output (z_t) is negatively associated with the changes in real interest rates:

$$z_t = -b_2 \left(i_t - E_t \pi_{t+1} - r^* \right) + u_{4t}, \qquad (7.4)$$

where i_t is the nominal interest rate, r^* is the target real interest rate, $u_{4t} \sim iid\left(0, \sigma_{u_4}^2\right)$, and $b_2 > 0$.

If the real interest rate, $i_t - E_t \pi_{t+1}$, is below the targeted real interest rate $[(i_t - E_t \pi_{t+1}) - r^* < 0]$, then agents increase their consumption and also raise output above the natural level ($z_t > 0$). The opposite occurs when the real interest rate is above the target.

7.2.2 The Taylor Rule

As in the previous chapters, we use a contemporaneous information Taylor rule:

$$i_t = \pi_t + \alpha_y z_t + \alpha_\pi \left(\pi_t - \pi^* \right) + r^*. \qquad (7.5)$$

Recall that policy is aggressive when both α_π and α_y are positive in (7.5). Positive values of α_π and α_y indicate a willingness to raise (lower) real interest in response to the positive (negative) deviations from either the target inflation rate ($\pi_t - \pi^*$), the output gap (z_t), or both.

7.3 Stability Analysis

We assume adaptive learning on the part of agents with respect to policymaker actions.[6] Our model has a unique and stable equilibrium (expectationally stable) when policymakers are aggressive in stopping inflation target deviations. Moreover, this equilibrium indicates that aggressive inflation-stabilizing policymaker behavior reduces inflation persistence.

We now examine whether the REE is determinate and dynamically stable. This analytical step provides the theoretical foundation that underlies policymakers' ability to steer, and ultimately anchor, the public's inflation forecasts to the target. The stability analysis proceeds in the following way.

7.3.1 The Equilibrium Inflation Rate

We first determine the reduced form for the inflation rate by substituting equation (7.5) into equation (7.4). We now solve for z_t, put that result into equation (7.3), and then solve that expression for π_t:

$$\pi_t = \Omega_0 + \Omega_1 \pi_{t-1} + \Omega_2 E_t \pi_{t+1} + \xi_t, \qquad (7.6)$$

[6] See the Appendix for a brief description of the adaptive learning approach. For more details see Evans and Honkapohja (2001).

where $\Omega_0 = \frac{a_2 b_2 \alpha_\pi \pi^*}{1+b_2\alpha_y+a_2b_2(1+\alpha_\pi)}$, $\Omega_1 = \frac{1+b_2\alpha_y}{2[1+b_2\alpha_y+a_2b_2(1+\alpha_\pi)]}$, $\Omega_2 = \frac{1+b_2\alpha_y+2a_2b_2}{2[1+b_2\alpha_y+a_2b_2(1+\alpha_\pi)]}$ and $\xi_t = \frac{a_2 u_{4t}+(1+b_2\alpha_y)u_{3t}}{1+b_2\alpha_y+a_2b_2(1+\alpha_\pi)}$. Equation (7.6) shows that current inflation depends on the first-order lag of inflation and also on expected future inflation.

We solve equation (7.6) and obtain the REE as

$$\pi_t = A + B\pi_{t-1} + \xi'_{t,} \qquad (7.7)$$

where $A = \frac{\Omega_0}{1-\Omega_2 B - \Omega_2}$, $B = \frac{1\pm\sqrt{1-4\Omega_1\Omega_2}}{2\Omega_2}$, and $\xi'_t = \frac{\xi_t}{1-\Omega_2 B}$.

Equation (7.7) is the minimum state variable (MSV) solution of inflation. This solution depends solely on the lagged inflation rate. We note further that equation (7.7) contains two possible MSV solutions (multiple equilibria) because the coefficient of lagged inflation, B, is a quadratic. We define the two values as $B^+ = \frac{1+\sqrt{1-4\Omega_1\Omega_2}}{2\Omega_2}$ and $B^- = \frac{1-\sqrt{1-4\Omega_1\Omega_2}}{2\Omega_2}$.

Here, we summarize the relation among policy, the Taylor principle, and the stable local solution:

Proposition 8. *For the reduced form in equation (7.7), B^- is a locally unique stationary solution for all $\alpha_\pi \geq 0$.*

Proof. To show that only B^- is less than 1 when $\alpha_\pi \geq 0$, we consider the values of α_π by separating it into two intervals: $\alpha_\pi = 0$ and $\alpha_\pi > 0$. When $\alpha_\pi = 0$, we have $B^+ = 1$

and $B^- = 1 - \frac{2b_2a_2}{1+2b_2a_2+b_2\alpha_y} < 1$. For the case of $\alpha_\pi > 0$, B^+ is a strictly increasing function. We show this result by taking the derivative of B^+ with respect to α_π:

$$\frac{\partial B^+}{\partial \alpha_\pi} = \frac{b_2a_2\left(1 + \Phi_{\alpha_\pi}\right)}{\left(1 + 2b_2a_2 + b_2\alpha_y\right)\Phi_{\alpha_\pi}} > 0 \quad \forall \alpha_\pi > 0,$$

where $\Phi_{\alpha_\pi} = \sqrt{1 - \frac{\left(1+b_2\alpha_y\right)\left(1+2b_2a_2+b_2\alpha_y\right)}{\left(1+b_2a_2(1+\alpha_\pi)+b_2\alpha_y\right)^2}}$.

On the other hand, B^- is a decreasing function when $\alpha_\pi > 0$ and asymptotically converges to zero. To see this result, we take the derivative of B^- with respect to α_π:

$$\frac{\partial B^-}{\partial \alpha_\pi} = \frac{b_2a_2\left(-1 + \Phi_{\alpha_\pi}\right)}{\left(1 + 2b_2a_2 + b_2\alpha_y\right)\Phi_{\alpha_\pi}} < 0 \quad \text{for } 0 \leq \alpha_\pi < \infty$$
$$= 0 \quad\quad\quad\quad\quad\quad \text{for } \alpha_\pi \to \infty,$$

and the limiting value of B^- as $\alpha_\pi \to \infty$ is zero:

$$\lim_{\alpha_\pi \to \infty} B^- = 0. \quad\quad\quad \blacksquare$$

Proposition 8 shows that B^- is a unique stationary solution when $\alpha_\pi \geq 0$. When policymakers adopt an aggressive policy rule, a stationary AR(1) solution can be obtained (i.e., B^-). However, an explosive AR(1) solution (i.e., B^+) would also be possible. This latter solution may cause the inflation rate to increase explosively (when $\pi_t - \pi_{t-1} > 0$) or may lead to a deflationary liquidity trap (when $\pi_t - \pi_{t-1} < 0$).

In the following section, we show that only the stationary solution (i.e., B^-) is attainable and that the explosive/liquidity trap solution (i.e., B^+) is not possible under adaptive learning (see McCallum 2003).[7]

7.3.2 Expectational Stability

Evans and Honkapohja (2001) present the general specification of equation (7.6) in the context of an adaptive learning model. They first assume that agents are able to obtain the current value of the inflation rate π_t at time t.

If we assume that agents learn in a manner consistent with recursive least squares, then we can summarize the stability of equation (7.7) in the following proposition:

---

[7] On the other hand, we also study the case of $\alpha_\pi < 0$ and find that the model can be determinate if $\frac{2(1+b_2\alpha_y)}{a_2 b_2} < \frac{(1+\alpha_\pi)^2}{-\alpha_\pi}$ is satisfied. This result implies that if the negative value of α_π is large enough (in an absolute sense), the model will have a unique stationary equilibrium. However, inflation persistence is bounded between zero and -1, which means that the level of inflation tends to oscillate in sign. This latter result is a mathematical curiosity and does not have any implication for our research questions.

Proposition 9. *For equation* (7.6), *the E-stability conditions for the MSV solutions are* $\Omega_1\Omega_2 (1 - \Omega_2 B)^{-2} < 1$ *and* $\Omega_2 (1 - \Omega_2 B)^{-1} < 1$. *If an MSV solution is stationary and E-stable, then it is locally stable under recursive least squares* (*RLS*) *learning (Evans and Honkapohja 2001).*

We note that the existence of the observable current value of the inflation rate π_t (at the time of expectations formation) creates a simultaneity problem (see Evans and Honkapohja 2001). To avoid this problem, we relax this assumption and instead assume that agents observe only the lagged inflation rate, π_{t-1}. This new assumption alters the E-stability conditions: B^+ is always unstable, but B^- is E-stable under the condition

$$-\sqrt{1 - 4\Omega_1\Omega_2} < 1 - 2\Omega_2. \tag{7.8}$$

Equation (7.8) is a necessary and sufficient condition for E-stability. In particular, if $\Omega_2 < \frac{1}{2}$, the MSV solution is sufficient for E-stability.

The E-stability condition is a basis for the policy implications of this book. The necessary and sufficient conditions for E-stability demonstrate the link among policymaker aggressiveness (adherence to the Taylor principle – α_π), agent learning, and inflation persistence. In equation (7.6), Ω_2 is less than half if $\alpha_\pi > 1$. This sufficient condition implies that agents are better able to learn the inflation equilibrium if policymakers aggressively stabilize inflation.

On the other hand, the necessary condition suggests a less vigorous response ($\alpha_\pi > 0$).

Proposition 10. *For equation* (7.6), *if agents do not observe the current value of the inflation rate* π_t *at the time of expectations formation, the MSV solution* (7.7) *is E-stable if* $\alpha_\pi > 0$.

Proof. This proposition is demonstrated by showing that the inequality in (7.8) holds. We first define the left-hand and right-hand sides in equation (7.8) as $LHS = -\sqrt{1 - 4\Omega_1 \Omega_2}$ and $RHS = 1 - 2\Omega_2$. Because we see from equation (7.6) that Ω_1 and Ω_2 are a function of α_y and α_π, we substitute the expressions of Ω_1 and Ω_2 into equation (7.8). It follows that $LHS = RHS$ when $\alpha_\pi = 0$. Further, LHS is monotonically decreasing over α_π, whereas RHS is monotonically increasing over α_π. We conclude that the condition in equation (7.8) holds if $\alpha_\pi > 0$. ∎

Figure 7.1 plots the values of LHS and RHS against α_π. The two curves intersect at $\alpha_\pi = 0$ and $LHS < RHS$ when $\alpha_\pi > 0$. Following Woodford (1999), the underlying parameters are

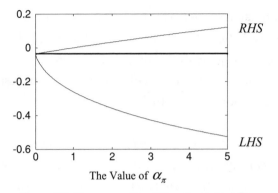

Figure 7.1 *Necessary Condition for E-Stability.*

$b_2 = 6.37$, $\alpha_y = 0.5$, and $a_2 = 0.024$. When $\alpha_\pi = 0$, $LHS = RHS = \frac{-a_2 b_2}{1 + b_2 \alpha_y + a_2 b_2} = -0.035243$.

7.4 Policy and Inflation Dynamics

7.4.1 Inflation Persistence

Equation (7.7) represents the AR(1) process of the inflation rate. Because B^+ is indeterminate and not E-stable, our empirical tests focus on the negative relation between α_π and B^-.

Proposition 11. *Provided that the model is determinate and E-stable, the persistence of inflation is reduced as policymakers*

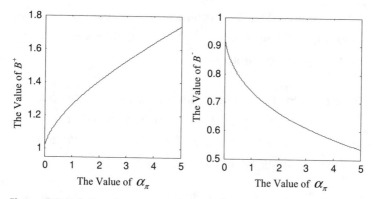

Figure 7.2 Relation between Inflation Persistence and Policy Rule Parameters.

respond aggressively ($\alpha_\pi > 0$) to the deviation of the inflation rate from its target.

Proof. We extend Proposition 8. Given that B^+ is not E-stable, we know that under the proof of Proposition 8, B^- decreases as α_π increases and B^- converges to 0 as α_π approaches ∞. ■

These results are presented in the left and right panels of Figure 7.2.

7.4.2 Inflation Volatility

We contend that inflation persistence and volatility are related, so inflation-stabilizing policy should also influence inflation volatility. We summarize the relation between inflation-stabilizing policy, α_π, and inflation volatility, σ_π^2, in the following proposition:

Proposition 12. *Provided that the model is determinate and E-stable, the variance of inflation is reduced as policymakers aggressively respond (i.e., follow the Taylor principle) to the deviation of the inflation rate from its target ($\alpha_\pi > 0$).*

Proof. From equation (7.7), we can solve for the variance of inflation σ_π^2:

$$\sigma_\pi^2 = \frac{\sigma_{\xi'}^2}{1 - (B^-)^2}, \tag{7.9}$$

where $\sigma_{\xi'}^2 = \frac{\sigma_\xi^2}{(1 - \Omega_2 B^-)^2}$.

Solving the expression of $\sigma_{\xi'}^2$, we have:

$$\sigma_{\xi'}^2 = \frac{4\left[a_2^2 \sigma_{u_2}^2 + \left(1 + b_2 \alpha_y\right)^2 \sigma_{u_1}^2\right]}{\left[1 + b_2 \alpha_y + a_2 b_2 \left(1 + \alpha_\pi\right)\right]^2 (1 + \Phi)^2}, \tag{7.10}$$

where $\Phi_{\alpha_\pi} = \sqrt{1 - \frac{(1 + b_2 \alpha_y)(1 + 2b_2 a_2 + b_2 \alpha_y)}{(1 + b_2 a_2 (1 + \alpha_\pi) + b_2 \alpha_y)^2}}$.

From Proposition 8, we show that $\frac{b_2 a_2}{1 + b_2 a_2 + b_2 \alpha_y} < \Phi_{\alpha_\pi} < 1$ for $\alpha_\pi \in [0, \infty)$ and B^- is less than 1 and decreases and approaches zero as α_π increases. This result implies that

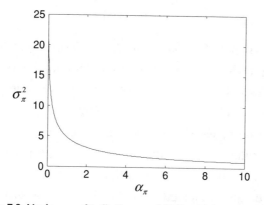

Figure 7.3 *Variance of Inflation and Policy Rule Parameters.*

$1 - \left(B^-\right)^2$ is bounded between $1 - \left(\frac{1-\alpha_y b_2}{1-\alpha_y b_2 + 2b_2 a_2}\right)^2$ and 1 for $\alpha_\pi \in [0, \infty)$. Therefore, we can see that σ_π^2 is a nonlinear decreasing function of α_π and asymptotically converges to zero as $\alpha_\pi \to \infty$. ∎

These results are presented in Figure 7.3.

Because we cannot observe current inflation in this model, B^- is the only valid result. It implies that an aggressive policy (i.e., $\alpha_\pi > 0$) helps agents learn the REE for inflation. In other words, the model demonstrates that a policy designed to achieve and maintain inflation stability reduces inflation persistence and, by extension, inflation volatility.

7.5 Tests

In their paper, Clarida et al. (2000) estimate a forward-looking Taylor rule for the period January 1960 through April 1996. They use Paul Volcker's appointment as Federal Reserve chairman in August 1979 to pinpoint a regime shift to a more aggressive inflation-stabilizing policy stance.[8] Their results show that the policy rule is significantly more aggressive about stabilizing inflation in the post-1979 period (hereafter referred to as Volcker-Greenspan) than in the pre-Volcker period.

According to our theory, inflation persistence should also be reduced significantly under an aggressive inflation-stabilizing policy. From our reduced form in equation (7.7), we estimate a first-order autoregressive process (i.e., AR[1]) of the U.S. inflation rate. As a consequence of the more aggressive inflation-stabilizing policy stance during the Volcker-Greenspan period (August 1979 through August 2000), we expect that the inflation-persistence parameter

---

[8] Recall from Chapter 3 that the policy shift to stricter monetary aggregate control was announced in early October 1979. This policy focus ended in October 1982. During this period, there was considerable volatility in short-term interest rates (see Figure 2.6 [federal funds rate]). There was also volatility in monetary aggregates as they followed a downward (restrictive) trend.

(B_t) in the Volcker-Greenspan period will be smaller than in the pre-Volcker period.

Consistent with our results in Chapter 2 on inflation forecasts and our narrative in Chapter 3, we also expect the aggressive inflation-stabilizing policy stance in the Volcker-Greenspan period to affect inflation persistence, but only after a lag. This relation reflects the public's adaptively learning the new (implicit) inflation target under the new policy environment. In addition, as we have discussed in our narrative, there were delays in 1979 and 1980 in sustaining the shift to inflation stability. Therefore, even though the Volcker-Greenspan period begins in the third quarter of 1979, we should not expect inflation persistence to decline until the early 1980s.

7.5.1 Estimates of Inflation Persistence

We base our analysis on quarterly observations of the inflation rate in the postwar United States (1960:I–2000:III). We use ordinary least squares (OLS) to estimate the persistence parameter (B_t) in equation (7.7). The first column in Table 7.1 reports the value of the persistence parameter over the full sample period. Columns 2 and 3 depict the pre-Volcker (1960:II–1979:II) and Volcker-Greenspan (1979:III–2000:III) eras, respectively.

Table 7.1. *Estimation of Inflation Persistence*

	Full Sample	Pre-Volcker	Volcker-Greenspan
Persistence Parameter, B_t	0.8202**	0.9070**	0.7452**
	(0.0629)	(0.0706)	(0.0988)
Chow Test F-statistic			2.2227
			(p-value = 0.1117)
R^2	0.67	0.74	0.62
No. of Observations	161	76	85

Note: Standard errors are reported in parentheses. ** indicates that the parameters are significant at the 1 percent level.

Using the full sample, the persistence parameter (B_t) equals 0.82 with a standard error of 0.06. The persistence parameter in the pre-Volcker period equals 0.91 with a standard error of 0.07. In contrast, the persistence parameter in the Volcker-Greenspan era equals 0.75 with a standard error of 0.1. The inflation rate is less persistent after Volcker is appointed as Fed chairman in August 1979.

To test whether inflation persistence is significantly reduced during the Volcker-Greenspan era, we use a Chow (1960) test. Not surprisingly, inflation persistence did not change. We find that the break-point period of 1979:III is not significant even at the 10 percent level.

This result makes sense because policy actions take effect with variable lags. Further, if agents learn adaptively we should expect a delay, particularly if the regime change reflects a substantial break with prior policy practices in the late 1960s and 1970s. Thus, we turn to an investigation of when policy does begin to have an effect, if ever, on inflation persistence and volatility.

7.5.2 The Appropriate Structural Break and Policy Effectiveness

There are many reasons for lags in public response to policy shifts. Explanations include the fact that there were no data at that time (about the new policymakers) for agents to use, as well as the credibility problems created by previous policymakers (Baxter 1985; Cukierman 1986; Granato 1996). With this in mind we ask this question: if 1979:III is the beginning of a shift in policymaker preferences (with the change of personnel), then when did policy eventually become effective in reducing the public's volatile inflation expectations? As Chapter 3 suggests, contemporary and historical accounts of this time suggest that monetary policy lacked sustained presidential administration support between August 1979 and December 1980.

Further volatility and uncertainty about policy actions came from the "monetarist experiment," in which the Federal Reserve targeted monetary aggregates for the first time (October 1979 to October 1982). We could surmise that the lack of experience with targeting monetary aggregates would lead to some initial instability.[9] These circumstances place the date for sustained and effective implementation of an aggressive policy in 1981 or 1982 (Kettl 1986; Greider 1987; Granato 1996; Clarida et al. 2000).

Figure 7.4 provides point estimates of inflation persistence (B_t) for a ten-year rolling sample starting in 1960:II. Most of our regressions show that inflation was highly persistent from 1960 to 1970 and 1970 to 1980. After 1980, inflation persistence starts falling. Further, we find the inflation persistence parameters from 1981 to 1991 and 1983 to 1993 are not significantly different from zero.

We also formulate a switching-regime regression model to estimate the break point for the full sample period (Quandt 1958; McGee and Carlton 1970; Hinkley 1971; Goldfeld and Quandt 1973; Owyang and Ramey 2002). Assuming that the error variances are equal for both regimes, we estimate two regime models by moving the different break-point periods from 1965:I to 1995:III (i.e., different partitions of the full sample period).

---

[9] Uncertainty about monetary aggregate movements was further compounded by the introduction of new components, such as NOW accounts (see Melton 1985).

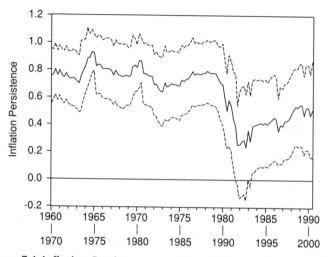

Figure 7.4 *Inflation Persistence over Time (10-year window rolling regression).*

We then examine the respective residual sums of squares and choose that break point for which this sum is the minimum. The minimum is 1981:IV. This finding coincides with contemporaneous and historical accounts (Kettl 1986; Greider 1987), as well as Chapter 3 (see Figure 7.5).

Andrews (1993) also develops a technique to test parameter instability and structural change with an unknown change point in the model (see also Piehl et al. 1999). Estimating equation (7.7), we find (see Figure 7.6) that the

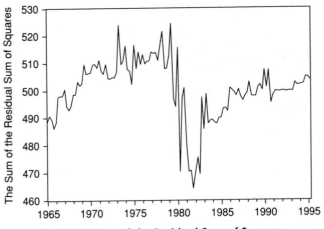

Figure 7.5 *Sum of the Residual Sum of Squares.*

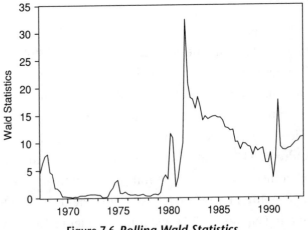

Figure 7.6 *Rolling Wald Statistics.*

Table 7.2. Estimation of Inflation Persistence with the Break Point of 1981:IV

	1960:II–1981:III	1981:IV–2000:III
Persistence Parameter, B_t	0.8830**	0.3631**
	(0.0687)	(0.1089)
Chow Test F-statistic	12.2096**	
R^2	0.76	0.17
No. of Observations	85	76

Note: Standard errors are reported in parentheses. ** indicates that the parameters are significant at the 1 percent level.

largest structural break exists in 1981:IV (sup Wald value = 32.35 [5 percent critical value = 7.93]).

We then reestimate the AR(1) model of inflation, using 1981:IV as the break point. In Table 7.2, the persistence parameter (B_t) of period 1960:II–1981:III equals 0.88 with a standard error of 0.06. However, for the period 1981:IV–2000:III persistence falls to 0.36 with a standard error equal to 0.1. Chow's structural break test shows that 1981:IV is significant at the 1 percent level.

In sum, after 1981:IV, inflation persistence drops significantly. This drop coincides with the aggressive and sustained monetary policy that takes effect in late 1981, and it is at this point, as opposed to the date of the Volcker appointment, that policy is effective. We also note that the R^2 of the second regression drops in Table 7.2 $(R^2 = 0.17)$. This reduction implies that, after 1981:IV, the lagged inflation rate loses relative explanatory power in the regression model.

7.5.3 Estimates of Inflation Persistence and Volatility

Autoregressive Conditional Heteroskedasticity (ARCH) Model Results. Here, we link both the variation and persistence of inflation. Prior work has looked exclusively at either persistence (Siklos 1999) or variability (Clarida et al. 2000). There is evidence that the mean and variance of inflation (σ_π^2) have a positive relation. For example, Figure 7.7 shows a positive relation between the persistence of inflation and its variance. To explore this mean-variance linkage further, we use an autoregressive conditional heteroskedasticity (ARCH) model to test whether an inflation-stabilizing policy reduces the variance of unexpected inflation (Ramey and Ramey 1995; Owyang 2001).

We estimate the ARCH representation as follows:

$$\pi_t = A + B\pi_{t-1} + C\sigma_{u,t}^2 + u_t, \qquad (7.11)$$

$$\sigma_{u,t}^2 = \varphi + \phi u_{t-1}^2 + \psi BP_t. \qquad (7.12)$$

From equation (7.11) u_t is the difference between inflation and the conditional (lagged) expected value of inflation

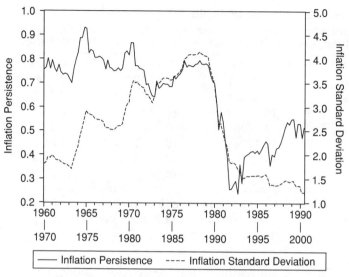

Figure 7.7 *Inflation Persistence and Volatility.*

(i.e., $u_t = \pi_t - E_{t-1}\pi_t$) which *can* be considered unexpected inflation. $\sigma^2_{u,t}$ is the conditional variance of u_t, given the value of lagged inflation (π_{t-1}). Thus, we treat this term $\sigma^2_{u,t}$ as the proxy for the unexpected inflation rate variance and predict that an aggressive inflation-stabilizing policy tack reduces $\sigma^2_{u,t}$ over time.[10] In equation (7.12), BP_t is a dummy variable for regime (policy) switches.

---

[10] From equation (7.7) one can show that aggressive monetary policy reduces the variance of ξ'_t.

Table 7.3. ARCH Model Results

Parameter	Baseline Model	Pre-/ Post-Volcker	1981:IV Break Point
B	0.7520**	0.7419**	0.6872**
	(0.0577)	(0.0560)	(0.0544)
C	0.3608*	0.3649*	0.3079**
	(0.1790)	(0.1744)	(0.0920)
ϕ	0.2706*	0.2723*	0.3227**
	(0.1224)	(0.1181)	(0.0880)
ψ	–	−0.1159	−1.3606*
	–	(0.5548)	(0.6062)

Note: Standard errors are reported in parentheses. * and ** indicate that the parameters are significant at the 5 percent and 1 percent levels, respectively.

Table 7.3 shows the results of the ARCH model when we use different break points. The first column represents the baseline model without a dummy variable. The coefficient of the unexpected inflation variance in equation (7.11) (C) equals 0.36 with a standard error equal to 0.17. The persistence parameter (B) equals 0.74 with a standard error equal to 0.05.

The variance of the unexpected inflation rate is positively related to its level. When we compare the ARCH results with the OLS estimation of the full sample in Table 7.1, we see that the persistence parameter in the ARCH model is smaller after we include the unexpected inflation variance.

However, it is still significantly different from zero at the 1 percent level.

The second column in Table 7.3 presents the results using a dummy variable for the Volcker and Volcker-Greenspan periods. Most parameters in equation (7.12) are significant at the 5 percent level or less. The exception is the parameter of the dummy variable (ψ).

This latter finding implies that there is no significant change in the unexpected inflation variance as of 1979:III. This result is consistent with our prior findings on policy implementation and the public's ability to learn adaptively and with a lag.

We then estimate the model with the break point of 1981:IV. The results reported in the last column indicate that all coefficients are significant at least at the 5 percent level. The change in regime during 1981 does have a negative effect on the variance of unexpected inflation, and it is large ($\psi = -1.36$ with a standard error equal to 0.6).

We also estimate the effect of regime changes on the persistence of inflation:

$$\pi_t = A' + B'\pi_{t-1} + C'\sigma_{u,t}^2 + D'BP_t + E'(BP_t * \pi_{t-1}) + u_t',$$

$$\tag{7.13}$$

$$\sigma_{u',t}^2 = \varphi' + \phi'u_{t-1}'^2 + \psi'BP_t. \tag{7.14}$$

Table 7.4. *ARCH Model Results with Structural Breaks*

Parameter	Pre-/ Post-Volcker	1981:IV Break Point
B'	0.8347**	0.9094**
	(0.0686)	(0.0802)
C'	0.2046**	0.2644$^+$
	(0.0663)	(0.1478)
D'	0.9655**	1.7577**
	(0.3768)	(0.4451)
E'	−0.3055**	−0.5132**
	(0.0982)	(0.1303)
ϕ'	0.6259**	0.3372**
	(0.2118)	(0.1440)
ψ'	−0.3911	−1.2276*
	(0.5156)	(0.6128)

Note: Standard errors are reported in parentheses. * and ** indicate that the parameters are significant at the 5 percent and 1 percent levels, respectively. $^+$ represents the *p*-value of C' of 0.0737.

Column 1 of Table 7.4 presents the results of the ARCH model with the pre-Volcker break-point dummy variable. Coefficients of B' and E' show the effect of regime switches on inflation persistence in the ARCH model. The persistence of inflation is reduced significantly during the Volcker and Greenspan era ($E' = -0.30$ with a standard error equal to 0.09). There is a positive effect of the variance of unexpected inflation on the inflation level ($C' = 0.20$ with a standard error equal to 0.06).

We also estimate the ARCH model using 1981:IV as the break point. Column 2 of Table 7.4 shows that most of the coefficients are significant at the 5 percent level. The coefficient of the unexpected inflation variance C' is between the 5 and 10 percent significance level (p-value $= 0.07$). The coefficient of the break point in equation (7.14) is negative and significant ($\psi' = -1.22$ with a standard error equal to 0.61). This result again shows that a significant reduction in the unexpected inflation variance occurred starting in 1981:IV.

7.6 Summary

This chapter considers the effect of an aggressive inflation-stabilizing policy on inflation persistence and volatility. We first develop a small-scale macroeconomic model of inflation and assume that agents learn about inflation in an adaptive manner (Evans and Honkapohja 2001). Under specific stability conditions, agents are able to learn the REE of inflation only if the policy rule stabilizes inflation. This result shows that aggressive inflation-stabilizing policies lower inflation persistence and volatility.

Using the postwar data in the United States for the period 1960:I–2000:III, we find that inflation persistence decreases over the sample period. We test for specific policy interventions that took an aggressive direction. The first policy intervention reflects the work of Clarida et al. (2000), who estimate a forward-looking policy rule before and after the appointment of Volcker as the chairman of the Federal Reserve. They find substantial differences in the estimated rule across periods, with the post-Volcker period being the most aggressive. However, this particular break point is not significant in our model.

One reason for this nonfinding is that the period of inflation control started between late 1981 or 1982, after policymakers could credibly implement such politically difficult policies (Kettl 1986; Granato 1996). The intuitive argument is that there are some political constraints that worked against earlier attempts to control inflation or led to a lag in implementing an aggressive inflation-stabilization policy.

Our results show that the persistence of inflation drops significantly starting sometime between late 1981 and the end of 1982 and continuing through the remainder of the sample period. The larger implication of this result points to the effectiveness of policy as opposed to luck.

As a final thought, we note that our model and results provide an alternative viewpoint on how policymakers behave. Many models of policymaker behavior tend to show that policymakers try to fool agents about the future course of policy. This temporary agent confusion has the effect of lowering unemployment or raising output in the near term. We turn that logic around and show that an aggressive inflation-stabilizing policy that achieves its (implicit or explicit) targets can have a salutary effect on agent expectations and thus contribute to IOCS.

7.7 Appendix to Chapter 7

7.7.1 A Brief Summary of the Adaptive Learning Approach

Here, we provide a brief introduction to adaptive learning and expectational stability developed by Evans (1985, 1989) and Evans and Honkapohja (1995, 2001). Instead of assuming that agents possess rational expectations, we assume that agents *learn* in an adaptive manner by forming expectations as new data become available. We then analyze the conditions of expectational stability (E-stability) under which the parameters in agents' forecasting rules – perceived law of motion (PLM) – are slowly adjusted to (or mapped to) the parameters in the actual law of motion (ALM), which can contain the REE. This E-stability condition determines whether agents are able to learn (locally) the correct forecasting rule – the REE.

Evans (1989) defines the E-stability condition in terms of the ordinary differential equation (ODE):

$$\frac{d\theta}{d\tau} = T(\theta) - \theta, \tag{7.15}$$

where θ is a finite dimensional parameter specified in the perceived law of motion, $T(\theta)$ is a mapping (so-called T-mapping) from the perceived to the actual law of motion, and τ denotes notional or artificial time. The REE, $\bar{\theta}$, corresponds to fixed points of $T(\theta)$. The stability condition of $\bar{\theta}$ is given under the following definition:

Definition 13. *$\bar{\theta}$ is expectationally stable (E-stable) if there exists $\varepsilon > 0$ such that $\theta(\tau) \to \bar{\theta}$ as $\tau \to \infty$, for all $\|\theta_0 - \bar{\theta}\| < \varepsilon$, where $\theta(\tau)$ is the trajectory that solves (7.15) subject to the initial condition $\theta(0) = \theta_0$.*

Evans and Honkapohja (2001) show that the notional time concept of expectational stability is generally consistent with the stability under real-time least squares learning. This correspondence is also called the *E-stability principle*.

Moreover, Evans and Honkapohja (2001) also mention that E-stability conditions are often easy to work out, but the convergence condition of adaptive learning involves a more technical analysis.

Least Squares Learning and Stochastic Recursive Algorithms. To see the general correspondence between E-stability and adaptive learning, we outline the technique of least squares learning and establish the condition of convergence[11] (see Bray 1982; Bray and Savin 1986; Marcet and Sargent 1989a, b). We assume that agents use recursive least squares (RLS) for updating their expectations each period up to the period $t - 1$:

$$y_t^e = \psi_{t-1}' x_{t-1}, \qquad (7.16)$$

and

$$\psi_t = \psi_{t-1} + t^{-1} R_t x_{t-1} \left(y_t - \psi_{t-1}' x_{t-1} \right), \qquad (7.17)$$
$$R_t = R_{t-1} + t^{-1} \left(x_{t-1} x_{t-1}' - R_{t-1} \right).$$

where x_t and y_t^e are $m \times 1$ vectors of independent and forecast-dependent variables, respectively; ψ_t is a $1 \times m$ coefficient vector updated by the system (7.17); and R_t denotes the moment matrix for x_t. Equation (7.16) represents

[11] See Evans and Honkapohja (2001) for further mathematical details.

agents' PLM that generates a corresponding ALM for y_t:

$$y_t = T\left(\psi_{t-1}\right)' x_{t-1} + v_t, \qquad (7.18)$$

where $v_t \sim iid\left(0, \sigma_v^2\right)$. When we substitute equation (7.18) into (7.17), we obtain the stochastic recursive system:

$$\psi_t = \psi_{t-1} + t^{-1} R_t x_{t-1}\left(x_{t-1}'\left(T\left(\psi_{t-1}\right) - \psi_{t-1}'\right) + v_t\right), \qquad (7.19)$$
$$R_t = R_{t-1} + t^{-1}\left(x_{t-1} x_{t-1}' - R_{t-1}\right).$$

We can also form the system (7.19) as a standard stochastic recursive algorithm (SRA) that determines the asymptotic stability for linear regression models:

$$\theta_t = \theta_{t-1} + \gamma_t Q\left(t, \theta_{t-1}, X_t\right),$$

where $\theta_t' = \left(vec\left(\psi_t\right), vec\left(R_{t+1}\right)\right)$, $X_t = \left(x_t, x_{t-1}, v_t\right)$, and $\gamma_t = t^{-1}$.

This SRA relates to the ODE:

$$\frac{d\theta}{d\tau} = h\left(\theta\left(\tau\right)\right), \qquad (7.20)$$

where the limit of $h\left(\theta\right)$ exists as:

$$h\left(\theta\right) = \lim_{t \to \infty} E Q(t, \theta, X),$$

where E represents the expectation of $Q\left(\cdot\right)$ with the fixed value of θ.

Following the set-up of the SRA, $\bar{\theta}$ is an equilibrium point if $h(\theta) = 0$ in equation (7.20). This result provides a standard mathematical definition of asymptotic stability for the differential equation:

Definition 14. $\bar{\theta}$ *is locally stable if for every $\varepsilon > 0$ there exists $\delta > 0$ such that $|\theta(t) - \bar{\theta}| < \varepsilon \ \forall \ |\theta(0) - \bar{\theta}| < \delta$. $\bar{\theta}$ is said to be locally asymptotically stable if $\bar{\theta}$ is stable and $\theta(\tau) \to \bar{\theta} \ \forall \ \theta(0)$ is somewhere in the neighborhood of $\bar{\theta}$.*

To show the local stability condition of $\bar{\theta}$, we compute the Jacobian matrix $Dh(\bar{\theta})$ and use the following lemma. This lemma is generally consistent with the concept of the E-stability condition:

Lemma 15. *If all eigenvalues of $Dh(\bar{\theta})$ have negative real parts, then $\bar{\theta}$ is a locally stable equilibrium point of $\frac{d\theta}{d\tau} = h(\theta)$. If some eigenvalues of $Dh(\bar{\theta})$ have a positive real part, then $\bar{\theta}$ is not a locally stable equilibrium point of $\frac{d\theta}{d\tau} = h(\theta)$.*

CHAPTER EIGHT

Inflation-Stabilizing Policy: Robustness

W e now examine whether an aggressive policy that puts greater relative emphasis on inflation stability is robust (see Wong and Wang 2005). Woodford (1999) has found that, under certain circumstances, inflation can exhibit explosive properties if policymakers follow an aggressive inflation-stabilizing policy. McCallum (2003) finds that Woodford's result lacks robustness when inflation persistence is factored. We build on McCallum's result and make a more general statement about the relation between inflation-stabilizing policy and inflation persistence and volatility.

We show that the condition for determinacy and learnability for the REE occurs when policymakers respond more aggressively to inflation target deviations. This finding provides a stronger argument in favor of the robustness of aggressive inflation-stabilizing policy – and the avoidance of explosive outcomes.[1]

8.1 The Model

As in Chapter 7, we have a three-equation model. We again assume a general contract model in which agents can use policy to gain accurate inflation forecasts when making plans:

$$\pi_t = (1 - \mu)\pi_{t-1} + \mu\delta E_t \pi_{t+1} + a_2 z_t + u_{5t}, \qquad a_2 > 0,$$

$$(8.1)$$

---

[1] In previous work, Bullard and Mitra (2001, 2002) evaluate the determinacy and learnability of an REE with alternative policy rules. They use a purely forward-looking model of the economy suggested by Woodford (1999) and combine that model with four alternative information structures of the Taylor rule: contemporaneous and lagged data, and forward-looking and contemporaneous expectations. Bullard and Mitra find that policy rules that respond relatively aggressively to inflation with little or no reaction to the output gap generally induce both determinate and learnable REE. In addition, when contemporaneous expectations are invoked, there exists a combination of nonaggressive inflation and output gap parameters (α_π, α_y) that produces both determinate and learnable REE outcomes. This result implies that the inflation and output gap parameters might be negative – $(\alpha_\pi, \alpha_y) < 0$ – and procyclical.

where π_t and z_t are the inflation rate and the output gap, respectively; $E_t\pi_{t+1}$ denotes the expected inflation rate over the next period; μ represents the weight of the expected inflation rate on the current inflation; δ is the household's discount factor; and $u_{5t} \sim iid\left(0, \sigma_{u_5}^2\right)$. All variables are expressed as deviations from a steady state.[2]

Equation (8.1) nests the specifications in Fuhrer (1995), Fuhrer and Moore (1995a), and Bullard and Mitra (2001, 2002) as special cases. Fuhrer (1995) and Fuhrer and Moore (1995a) assume a two-period contract model in which the market price is expressed as the average of the current and the lagged contract wages. Because agents are concerned with their real wages over the lifetime of their contract, they derive the price-setting rule of equation (8.1) where $\mu = 1/2$. On the other hand, Bullard and Mitra (2001, 2002) follow the set-up in Woodford (1999) and rely solely on the forward-looking component of inflation, $E_t\pi_{t+1}$. Therefore, equation (8.1) can be reduced to a special case when $\mu = 1$.

---

[2] Fuhrer (1995) and Fuhrer and Moore (1995a) do not set up their model as a deviation from a steady state. However, the model can be derived in that form without changing the equations being considered here.

As in equation (7.4), we consider a version of the IS curve that we derive from the Euler equation for consumer utility maximization (McCallum and Nelson 1999; Woodford 1999):

$$z_t = -b_2 \left(i_t - E_t \pi_{t+1} - r^* \right) + b_3 E_t z_{t+1} + u_{6t}, \qquad b_2, b_3 > 0, \tag{8.2}$$

where i_t is the nominal interest rate, r^* is the target real interest rate, and $u_{6t} \sim iid \left(0, \sigma_{u_6}^2 \right)$. As before, we use a contemporaneous information Taylor rule specified in (7.5).

To solve the system, we substitute (7.5) into (8.2) and solve for π_t and z_t, using the following form:

$$q_t = A + B E_t q_{t+1} + C q_{t-1} + \zeta_t, \tag{8.3}$$

where $q_t = \begin{bmatrix} \pi_t \\ z_t \end{bmatrix}$, $A \equiv W \begin{bmatrix} 0 \\ \pi^* \alpha_\pi b_2 \end{bmatrix}$, $B \equiv W \begin{bmatrix} \delta\mu & 0 \\ b_2 & b_3 \end{bmatrix}$,

$C \equiv W \begin{bmatrix} 1 - \mu & 0 \\ 0 & 0 \end{bmatrix}$, $\zeta_t \equiv W \begin{bmatrix} u_{5t} \\ u_{6t} \end{bmatrix}$, and

$$W = \begin{bmatrix} 1 & -a_2 \\ b_2 \left(1 + \alpha_\pi \right) & 1 + b_2 \alpha_y \end{bmatrix}^{-1}.$$

8.2 Determinacy

We consider whether the REE is unique in this model. We first eliminate the constant term A by taking the difference from the mean value of equation (8.3):

$$\tilde{q}_t = B E_t \tilde{q}_{t+1} + C \tilde{q}_{t-1} + \zeta_t, \tag{8.4}$$

where $\tilde{q}_t = q_t - \bar{q}$ and $\bar{q} = (I - B - C)^{-1} A$.

Then we rearrange equation (8.4):

$$
\begin{bmatrix} 1 & 0 & -C_{11} \\ 0 & 1 & -C_{21} \\ 1 & 0 & 0 \end{bmatrix}
\begin{bmatrix} \tilde{\pi}_t \\ \tilde{z}_t \\ \tilde{\pi}_t^L \end{bmatrix}
=
\begin{bmatrix} B_{11} & B_{12} & 0 \\ B_{21} & B_{22} & 0 \\ 0 & 0 & 1 \end{bmatrix}
\begin{bmatrix} \tilde{\pi}_{t+1} \\ \tilde{z}_{t+1} \\ \tilde{\pi}_{t+1}^L \end{bmatrix} \tag{8.5}
$$

$$
+ \begin{bmatrix} \zeta_{1t} \\ \zeta_{2t} \\ 0 \end{bmatrix}
- \begin{bmatrix} B_1' \\ B_2' \\ 0 \end{bmatrix} \eta_{t+1},
$$

where $\tilde{\pi}_t^L \equiv \tilde{\pi}_{t-1}$, $C \equiv \begin{bmatrix} C_{11} & C_{12} \\ C_{21} & C_{22} \end{bmatrix}$, $B \equiv \begin{bmatrix} B_{11} & B_{12} \\ B_{21} & B_{22} \end{bmatrix} \equiv$

$\begin{bmatrix} B_1' \\ B_2' \end{bmatrix}$, $\zeta_t \equiv \begin{bmatrix} \zeta_{1t} \\ \zeta_{2t} \end{bmatrix}$, $E_t \tilde{q}_{t+1} = \tilde{q}_{t+1} - \eta_{t+1}$ and $\eta_t \sim iid\left(0, \sigma_\eta^2\right)$.

Taking the inverse of the left-hand side matrix and multiplying the matrix associated with the one-time-period forward variables gives us:

$$
J = \begin{bmatrix}
0 & 0 & 1 \\
\dfrac{b_2}{1+b_2\alpha_y} & \dfrac{b_3}{1+b_2\alpha_y} & -\dfrac{b_2(1+\alpha_\pi)}{1+b_2\alpha_y} \\
\dfrac{\mu(1+b_2\alpha_y)+b_2a_2}{(1+b_2\alpha_y)(-1+\mu)} & \dfrac{a_2b_3}{(1+b_2\alpha_y)(-1+\mu)} & -\dfrac{1+b_2a_2+b_2a_2\alpha_\pi+b_2\alpha_y}{(1+b_2\alpha_y)(-1+\mu)}
\end{bmatrix}.
$$

In equation (8.5), $\tilde{\pi}_t$ and $\tilde{z}_t$ are free endogenous variables, but $\tilde{\pi}_t^L$ is a predetermined endogenous variable. We need to have exactly two of the eigenvalues of J inside the unit circle for uniqueness. We provide the condition for determinacy in the following proposition.

Proposition 16. *According to the model in equation* (8.3), *where* $\mu \in (0, 1)$, *the necessary and sufficient condition for a unique REE is:*

$$
a_2\alpha_\pi + (1 - \delta)\,\mu\alpha_y > 0, \tag{8.6}
$$

and

$$
\alpha_y > -1/b_2. \tag{8.7}
$$

Proof. We calculate the characteristic polynomial for the inverse matrix of J and get:

$$
p(L) = \{(L-1)(Lb_2a_2 + Lb_3 - 1) - (L^2\delta - 1)(Lb_3 - 1)\mu
$$
$$
- Lb_2a_2\alpha_\pi + b_2[1 - \mu + L(L\delta\mu - 1)]\alpha_y\}/\delta b_3\mu.
$$

Note that $p(1) < 0$, $p(0) > 0$, and $p(-1) > 0$. By Descartes' rule of signs (Barbeau 1989), there is necessarily a positive root and either two negative roots or a pair of complex conjugates. $p(1) < 0$ and $p(-1) > 0$ if (8.6) is satisfied. $p(0) > 0$ holds by condition (8.7). ∎

According to the general relative-real-wage contracting specification in equation (8.1), we include a lagged inflation term in convex combination with the expected inflation term. Because μ represents the relative weight between lagged and expected inflation, $\mu \to 1$ nests the determinacy condition in Bullard and Mitra's (2002) model.

For the case of $\mu \in (0, 1)$, Proposition 16 tells us that in an economy with inflation persistence, the policy rule must use a larger response parameter in relation to inflation target deviations (or for both inflation target and output gap deviations) if it is to attain a unique REE.

This result provides a stronger stability condition than the ones in Bullard and Mitra (2001, 2002). On the other hand, if the lagged inflation component dominates in the model (that is, $\mu \to 0$), the necessary and sufficient condition for determinacy requires that $\alpha_\pi > 0$. Regardless of these nuances, these findings indicate that policy must be aggressive enough in responding to inflation target deviations.

8.3 Adaptive Learning by Agents

Although the REE is determinate, it is also important to see whether agents are able to learn the REE. In this section, we analyze the expectational stability (E-stability) condition in this model. As we did in Chapter 7, we also assume that agents make their forecasts by using recursive least squares.[3]

Now, suppose that agents believe that inflation and the output gap follow the process (PLM):

$$q_t = c_{t-1} + d_{t-1}q_{t-1} + e_{t-1}\zeta_t, \tag{8.8}$$

where c_t, d_t, and e_t are the coefficients updated by running RLS, using actual data (i.e., $[1, q_{t-1}, \zeta_t]$) available over time. As in Chapter 7, we assume that the current value of the endogenous variable q_t is not available at the time of the formation of expectations. This assumption eliminates any simultaneity problem. The expected value of q_{t+1} at time t is:

$$E_t q_{t+1} = (c_{t-1} + d_{t-1}c_{t-1}) + d_{t-1}^2 q_{t-1} + d_{t-1}e_{t-1}\zeta_t, \tag{8.9}$$

---

[3] See Appendix in Chapter 7 for a brief description of the adaptive learning approach.

Inserting equation (8.9) into equation (8.3), we can solve for the *actual law of motion*, or *ALM*, implied by the PLM:

$$q_t = (A + Bc_{t-1} + Bd_{t-1}c_{t-1}) + \left(Bd_{t-1}^2 + C\right)q_{t-1}$$
$$+ (Bd_{t-1}e_{t-1} + I)\,\zeta_t. \tag{8.10}$$

We define the mapping (*T-Mapping*) from the PLM to the ALM as:

$$T\begin{pmatrix} c \\ d \\ e \end{pmatrix} = \begin{pmatrix} A + Bc + Bdc \\ Bd^2 + C \\ Bde + I \end{pmatrix}. \tag{8.11}$$

We obtain the E-stability conditions by deriving the differential equation from equation (8.11). Using the rules for vectorization of matrix products (see Magnus and Neudecker 1999), we have:

$$DT_c\left(\bar{c}, \bar{d}\right) = B\left(I + \bar{d}\right)$$
$$DT_d\left(\bar{d}\right) = \bar{d}' \otimes B + I \otimes B\bar{d}$$
$$DT_e\left(\bar{d}, \bar{e}\right) = B\bar{d}. \tag{8.12}$$

Equation (8.12) gives us the following result:

Proposition 17. *An MSV solution $\bar{c}$, $\bar{d}$, $\bar{e}$ to equation (8.3) is E-stable when all eigenvalues of the matrices $DT_c\left(\bar{c}, \bar{d}\right)$, $DT_d\left(\bar{d}\right)$,*

$DT_e\left(\bar{d}, \bar{e}\right)$ *given by equation (8.12) have real parts less than 1. The solution is not E-stable when any of the eigenvalues has a real part greater than 1 (Evans and Honkapohja 2001).*

Using baseline parameters suggested by Woodford (1999) and Bullard and Mitra (2001, 2002), we illustrate our results in Figure 8.1.[4] We show that the E-stability condition is consistent with the determinacy condition (8.6). Figure 8.1 also shows how the value of μ changes both the determinacy and E-stability conditions.

There are three cases: Bullard and Mitra's model ($\mu \to 1$), Fuhrer and Moore's (1995a) model ($\mu = 1/2$), and a case without a forward-looking component ($\mu \to 0$). Figure 8.1 plots the regions of determinacy and expectation stability as a function of α_π and α_y in the above cases.

In the region where $\alpha_\pi > 0$, the REE is determinate and E-stable in all cases. However, the region of indeterminacy and E-instability in Fuhrer and Moores' specification ($\mu = 1/2$) is larger than that in Bullard and Mitra's set-up (without the component of inflation persistence [$\mu \to 1$]).

---

[4] According to Woodford (1999) and Bullard and Mitra (2002), $a_2 = 0.024$, $b_2 = 6.37$, and $b_3 = 1$.

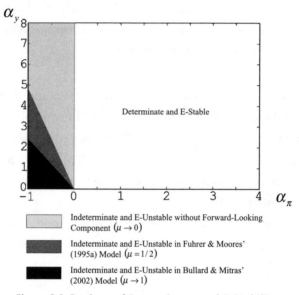

Figure 8.1 *Regions of Determinacy and E-Stability.*

This result suggests that, if inflation persistence exists in an economy, then policymakers should use larger inflation target deviation and output target/gap parameters (α_π, α_y) in the policy rule so that the REE can be determinate and learnable for the public. Moreover, if inflation in an economy is affected solely by lagged inflation $(\mu \to 0)$, then policymakers must be aggressive in attaining their inflation target if they are to satisfy the determinacy and learnability condition. Taken as a whole, these results indicate there is a much broader and robust implication from an aggressive, inflation-stabilizing policy.

8.4 Model Illustrations

8.4.1 Learning Dynamics

We now illustrate the learning dynamics of our model. Recall we assume that agents make their forecasts under least squares learning. We apply the technique of Evans and Honkapohja (2001) to simulate equations (8.3) and (8.13):

$$\begin{bmatrix} \pi_t \\ z_t \end{bmatrix} = \begin{bmatrix} c_{1,t-1} \\ c_{2,t-1} \end{bmatrix} + \begin{bmatrix} d_{11,t-1} & d_{12,t-1} \\ d_{21,t-1} & d_{22,t-1} \end{bmatrix} \begin{bmatrix} \pi_{t-1} \\ z_{t-1} \end{bmatrix} + e_{t-1}\zeta_t.$$

(8.13)

With the baseline parameters,[5] the REE is $\bar{c}_1 = 0.045$, $\bar{c}_2 = 0.210$, $\bar{d}_{11} = 0.776$, $\bar{d}_{12} = 0$, $\bar{d}_{21} = -1.050$, and $\bar{d}_{22} = 0$. The

[5] We set $\mu = 0.5$, $\delta = 0.99$, and $\alpha_\pi = \alpha_y = 0.5$ in this simulation.

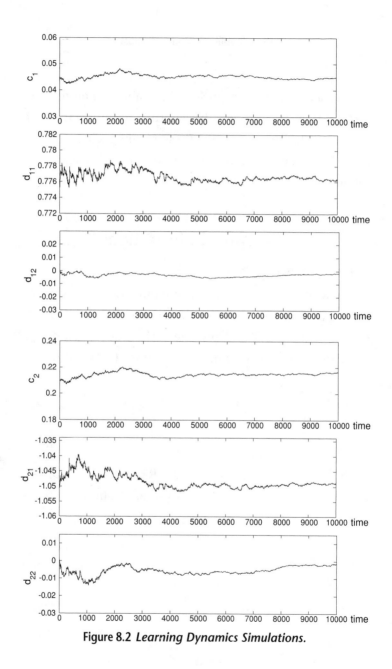

Figure 8.2 *Learning Dynamics Simulations.*

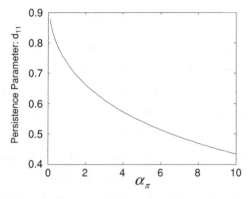

Figure 8.3 *Persistence Parameter vs. α_π.*

results in Figure 8.2 show that $c_{1,t-1}$, $d_{11,t-1}$, $d_{12,t-1}$, $c_{2,t-1}$, $d_{21,t-1}$, and $d_{22,t-1}$ all converge to the REE over time.

8.4.2 Inflation Persistence

We can also show that an inflation-stabilizing policy affects inflation persistence. In equation (8.13), d_{11} represents the AR(1) process of the inflation rate. Figure 8.3 shows that, when we use the baseline parameters above, an increase in α_π reduces inflation persistence. This result also supports the argument in Chapter 7, in which we find that the aggressive inflation-stabilizing policy stance in the early 1980s corresponded with a substantial reduction in inflation persistence in the ensuing years.

8.5 Summary

This chapter demonstrates the robustness of an inflation-stabilizing policy for a general contract model containing inflation persistence. On an intuitive level, an aggressive inflation-stabilizing policy stance steers the public to make more accurate inflation forecasts. The public adjusts its plans to fit this reality, thereby encouraging IOCS. As discussed in Chapter 7, the public learns, while making its plans, to substitute the policymakers' (implicit or explicit) inflation target for the past history of inflation.

We show this dynamic by extending the Bullard and Mitra (2001, 2002) study on the determinacy and learnability of an REE when policymakers follow a Taylor rule. Our model demonstrates a stronger, more robust result for aggressive inflation-stabilizing policy than the ones given by Bullard and Mitra (2001, 2002). We show that, if inflation is more persistent in an economy, the policy rule parameters (α_π, α_y) should have larger values (be more aggressive), so that the AR(1) REE is determinate and learnable.

CHAPTER NINE

Conclusion and Implications

The central theme of this book is that a macroeconomic policymaker's role is to enhance the public's ability to coordinate its information, expectations, and economic activities.
We narrow the focus of information coordination to policymaker efforts to minimize public uncertainty about current
and future inflation. If policymakers take actions to attain a
specific inflation rate – and consistently achieve this target –
then the public will learn to incorporate this value as its inflation expectation. At the macroeconomic level, we argue
that this added certainty in future inflation aids in the stability of future plans and, ultimately, leads to what we have
called IOCS.

The findings are wide ranging. In Part I, starting with
Chapter 2, we used basic statistical analysis to illustrate the
macroeconomic stability and instability in the United States

since 1960. We find that both inflation and output stability (IOCS) coexisted for a significant part of this 41-year period.

In particular, IOCS occurred (roughly speaking) for the periods 1962–9 and 1985–2000, periods that coincided with the longest economic expansions since 1854. Furthermore, because IOCS depends on the coordination of price information, we also examine the ability of the public to make and learn correct inflation forecasts. We find that increasing inflation forecast accuracy coincided with periods of IOCS.

Another issue in Chapter 2 is to illustrate whether key policy indicators share periodic patterns that coincide with periods of IOCS. To establish a link between policy and IOCS we use the following indicators: the federal funds rate ratio, the Taylor rule (Taylor principle), and Taylor principle deviations (volatility).

Taken altogether, the policy and economic indicators reveal some important patterns.[1] These relations between policy and economic indicators appeared in the mid-1960s, the mid- to late 1970s, and the early 1980s. The changes in

---

[1] Recall that in Chapter 2, we found that forecast errors were most volatile during non-IOCS periods. We find that this inflation uncertainty was also shared by policymakers.

the policy indicators preceded and accompanied cyclical patterns in inflation and output volatility (IOCS) and also surveyed inflation expectations and inflation forecast errors.

Starting in the mid-1960s, policy indicators (in general) showed a gradual movement toward deemphasizing inflation stability. The federal funds rate ratio, for example, began a nearly continuous decline. This drop reflected the failure to raise short-term interest rates to stem a gradual surge in inflation. Policymakers tolerated a low nominal (and real) interest rate. The Taylor rule showed a similar pattern, exhibiting an inflationary (even procyclical) policy stance.

By the late 1960s and early 1970s, economic indicators began to reflect greater volatility. Inflation forecasts exhibited larger means, which reflected the gradual and tolerated increases in inflation.

We also show that the volatility in inflation, output, and inflation forecast errors started to increase. From the mid- to late 1970s, policy continued to deemphasize inflation stability, and economic indicators became increasingly volatile. Inflation forecasts continued to reflect the increasing level of inflation. Violent cyclical swings in inflation and output volatility and in inflation forecast errors occurred with successively greater severity. For the most part, there was little evidence of a sustained inflation-stabilizing countercyclical policy during much of the 1970s.

However, beginning in the early 1980s, there was a decided change toward an aggressive inflation-stabilizing policy. This policy shift has been maintained in the ensuing years. By the mid-1980s, the overall volatility of all economic indicators began to drop precipitously. IOCS returned to levels consistent with the early to mid-1960s, a period that, by most of our indicators, also witnessed inflation-stabilizing policy.

Given the basic statistical similarity in the periodic changes in policy and IOCS, our next step was to examine the historical events and their interaction with changes in scientific doctrine. We wanted to see whether policy shifts presented in Chapter 2 reflected shifting policymaker attitudes toward inflation stabilization.

Chapter 3 summarizes similarities in many historical accounts. Chief among our findings is the evolution of policymaker thinking about the Phillips curve. In the early 1960s, policymakers adopted the view that there was a permanent trade-off between inflation and unemployment. This view led them to believe that expansionary policy could permanently reduce unemployment with little cost. In the late 1960s, Friedman and Phelps challenged the scientific consensus. Only at the beginning of the 1980s did policy-makers implement the Friedman and Phelps argument.

We contend that the mix of economic events and scientific doctrine has been largely responsible for the major policy shifts since 1960, policy shifts that have created both harmful and beneficial business cycle outcomes. On the harmful side, the stagflation of the 1970s was associated with the reduced policy emphasis (in the mid- to late 1960s and 1970s) on inflation stability. We contrast these adverse outcomes with what went right: the reemergence of an inflation-stabilizing policy emphasis that was associated with IOCS and the economic expansions of the 1980s and 1990s.

Part II of the book develops a small-scale macroeconomic model to identify linkages between policy and IOCS. In Chapter 5, we explore the stability of both inflation and output and their relation to policy. We find no evidence of a permanent trade-off between inflation and output stability. IOCS can be achieved up to a point. There is a trade-off between inflation and output variability, but this trade-off occurs when policy parameters (countercyclical actions) appear to be quite large.

In Chapter 6, we extend the aggregate findings to policymaker preferences. Using a well-defined loss function, we explore optimal policymaker actions. We find that the only permanent trade-off that exists in our model is between interest rate variability and inflation and output variability (Fuhrer and Moore 1995). Although IOCS can be attained, it is clear that an aggressive inflation-stabilizing policy tack is not without cost.

We then conduct more rigorous statistical analysis of this trade-off between IOCS and interest rate volatility.[2] Using VAR, we find that both inflation and output stability are significantly and negatively related to the volatility of the Taylor principle deviation. The results indicate that inflation volatility responds to interest rate volatility first, peaking at five quarters. Output volatility responds to interest rate volatility later, beginning at about three quarters, with the peak effect occurring at about ten quarters. These findings support the view that the trade-off between inflation and output volatility is less of a "permanent" trade-off than is the trade-off between IOCS and interest rates.

---

[2] Prior research finds a trade-off between inflation and output stability when a given policy target is followed (Taylor 1979, 1994). In the ensuing years, efforts have been geared to refining the conditions in which the inflation-output volatility trade-off occurs. For example, Svensson (2003a) shows that the trade-off depends on the persistence in the output gap and on whether policy targets inflation or the price level.

A final issue in Chapter 6 is the influence that economic shocks have on the feasible range of parameters (counter-cyclical actions) that lead to IOCS outcomes. We find that demand shocks provide a broader range of inflation-stabilizing policymaker actions (parameter range is larger), but that in the case of supply shocks, a large and aggressive policy tack eventually leads to trade-offs between inflation and output stability. In other words, the range of feasible policy responses is smaller when supply shocks occur.

In Part III we shift our focus to coordination dynamics between policymakers and the public. If our theory is correct, then when agents are making inflation forecasts, inflation-stabilizing policy should encourage them to gradually substitute the policymakers' (implicit or explicit) inflation target for the agents' use of the past history of inflation. Econometrically speaking, the persistence of inflation should dissipate during periods when policymakers follow an inflation-stabilizing policy and information coordination is evident.

In Chapter 7, we use data in the United States for the period 1960:I–2000:III, and we find that inflation persistence decreased over the sample period. When we test for specific policy interventions, we find evidence that inflation persistence has fallen when credible inflation-stabilizing policy has been maintained.

This issue of policy robustness is examined in Chapter 8. Using a model with fairly general properties (in comparison to others in the literature), we find that aggressive application of the Taylor rule (the Taylor principle) avoids liquidity traps (deflation) because our REE is E-stable and learnable, whereas liquidity traps are explosive and unlearnable.

9.1 Implications for Policymakers

We agree with Blinder (1998) that our ideas presented here "do not provide pat answers for central bankers" and that our technical approach "cannot be applied mechanically" (p. 22). However, we specify and extend a framework about the theory of economic policy – how it can work and the benefits it creates. Our work suggests that, if monetary policymakers take their role as being one that is focused on coordinating information, then they should enact policies that stabilize both inflation and output; however, inflation stability should be the first goal among equals. The added emphasis on inflation stability supports our view that countercyclical (stabilization) policy works best when it is intended to improve the coordination of price information.

9.1.1 Institutional Reform and Information Coordination

There are numerous issues pertaining to institutional reform and the implementation of policy. These factors are spelled out elsewhere (see, for example, Bernanke et al. 1999; Faust and Henderson 2004). In terms of specific institutional reforms, we agree with Siklos (2002) when he states that "mechanisms must be put in place to ensure that objectives are clearly explained to the public. The latter requires adequate disclosure of policy decisions and the means by which they were reached" (pp. 306–307).

These mechanisms include rules for striking a balance between policymaker accountability[3] and policymaker autonomy.[4] On the one hand, policymaker accountability can lead to greater transparency and speed in the public disclosure of

---

[3] Siklos (2002: 228) characterizes policymaker accountability as containing such characteristics as the clarity of stated objectives, the forms of communication in which policy decisions are transmitted to the public, and the degree to which (and to whom) the monetary authority is held responsible for its actions.

[4] See Siklos (2002: 247–256) for a summary of measurable factors in policymaker accountability and policymaker autonomy.

policymaker goals and targets, as well as the information used to arrive at these decisions.

Note, however, that there is no free lunch with various reforms. Institutional reforms typically involve a tension between policymaker accountability and policymaker autonomy (i.e., central bank independence). The very characteristics of accountability that can assist in enhancing information coordination can also create political tensions that lead to legislative and executive threats and actions that reduce policymaker autonomy. In addition, policymaker autonomy is an important factor in allowing policymakers to take the sometimes necessary and difficult steps to maintain inflation stability. Yet, our analysis also suggests that, even when policymaker autonomy exists (by statute), it is not sufficient to prevent the deemphasis of inflation stability as a policy goal. The Federal Reserve has, by international standards, substantial autonomy, yet inflation stability was deemphasized for substantial periods of time.

The practical policy message in this book is *strategic* – as opposed to tactical – in specifying a specific mix of institutional and procedural features. We would argue that there is more than one way to ensure that policymakers can fulfill their role as information coordinator. Once policymakers view their role in this light, all other practical questions can be directed to that end. Procedures and institutions can be structured and restructured with information coordination in mind.

We also recognize that no policy is implemented with complete certainty. Policy implementation is a complicated process based on imperfect information pertaining to problem recognition, the effects of policy, and even shifts in policymaker preferences.[5] Imperfect information challenges can manifest themselves in many ways. For example, despite the utility of inflation targets, there are still important considerations of (mis)measurement (Alchian and Klein 1973). Too narrow or too broad a measure could create policy responses that could impair the coordination of information.

Yet another concern about policy implementation deals with how fast and how high interest rates should be raised or lowered. Consistent with our strategic goal of coordinating price information, we argue that interest rates should

---

[5] Add to these complications the fact that there is no agreement about the correct macroeconomic model or the magnitude of various variables or parameters (see Blinder 1998: 9–13). As Part II of this book shows, there are uncertainties about the various targets (inflation and natural [potential] rate of output), the magnitude of the real interest rate, and the actual trade-off between inflation and output variability.

respond in a manner that is most consistent with maintaining information coordination (i.e., minimizing public forecast errors).[6] The Taylor principle is related to this criterion, and we think it is a good reference point. However, there may be circumstances, such as a response to alternative exogenous shocks (see Chapter 6), that could make the Taylor principle the wrong choice. We contend that the Taylor rule and the Taylor principle are best suited in helping policymakers fulfill their role as coordinators of price information, but (consistent with our statement above) if there are alternatives that can facilitate information coordination in a more efficient way, then they should be adopted.

What we are suggesting is that, despite these complications, policy does evolve and we find that policymakers can correct their mistakes. That is one lesson drawn from our historical analysis in Chapter 3 on the policy deemphasis and reemphasis of inflation stability. Further, when the overriding strategic role of information coordination is maintained, changes will be made that further progress, and more important, reduce errors.

---

[6] For further empirical and theoretical research on this question of how fast and how high interest rates have been raised see Levin, Wieland, and Williams (1999), Woodford (1999), Clarida et al. (2000), and Sack and Wieland (2000).

9.2 Implications for Future Research

One of the most important lines of future research will be to address the link between aggressive inflation-stabilizing policy and IOCS. The evaluation procedures for IOCS spelled out in this book require extensive empirical corroboration. On the theoretical side, there is substantial work on the mix of institutions, accountability mechanisms, and information transparency, but these have not been applied to the theme and model in this book.[7]

9.2.1 The Need for Comparative Analysis

A chief problem in finding evidence for or against IOCS is that each point in the policy space associated with crossover effects (CEOT, CEIT) is associated with a particular policy under a specific set of circumstances. Because we have only examined the United States and only for the period 1960–2000, the model and results require far greater inquiry (see Cecchetti and Ehrmann 1999/2002).

---

[7] On these institutional, accountability, and information issues, we note the work of Debelle and Fischer (1994), Bernanke and Woodford (1997), Romer and Romer (1997), Svensson (1997), Bernanke et al. (1999), Drazen (2000), Persson and Tabellini (2000), Freeman (2002), and Siklos (2002).

A multicountry study could improve our understanding of the policy-IOCS relation along the following lines. In the first instance, countries that have similar policymaking institutions and that face similar economic circumstances can provide sufficient control to help isolate policy-IOCS combinations. At the other extreme, the differences among countries also present an opportunity to further our understanding. This variability in policy actions, economic structure, economic outcomes, and political-economic history could add to an expanded analysis and provide alternative mechanisms (conditions) to determine IOCS outcomes.[8]

9.2.2 The Effect of Political and Social Forces on Policy

Our research can also be extended to include the potential political and social forces that influence policy. Our analysis starts in the middle of the policy and outcome process (abstracting out fiscal policy) and traces the various

[8] One important issue in a comparative analysis would be the variability in policy autonomy of the monetary authority. In less autonomous policy settings, fiscal policy – for example, monetizing debt – can have a substantial influence on whether policymakers can take actions to stabilize inflation.

empirical implications.[9] However, much work remains to be done in finding the mix of political and social factors that facilitates and encourages what we have argued is the optimal role for a policymaker. A particular concern is the relationship between the public and policymakers. There are many studies on monetary policy games (see Cukierman and Meltzer 1986), but we believe that an approach that allows for public and policymaker learning could provide new insights. This interaction between the public and policymakers bears on the policymakers' role because public learning has the potential to constrain policymaker discretion.[10] In more technical terms, we think that these avenues of inquiry could lead to finding

[9] Integrating fiscal policy would be an important avenue of inquiry. For ways of characterizing fiscal policy see, for example, Drazen (2000) and Persson and Tabellini (2000).

[10] In a dynamic setting in which the issue is how quickly citizens learn rational expectations equilibria, we find informational rigidities occur even in cases in which a subset of the population has complete information (see Kandel and Zilberfarb 1999; Granato and Wong 2005).

In related work, Sargent (1999), Gavin and Mandal (2001), Lansing (2001), and Orphanides and Williams (2003b, 2004) have some promising results, but their emphasis is on how policymakers learn about economic outcomes. Svensson (2003b) provides a summary of some of these developments.

conditions that create upper and lower bounds for the parameters α_π and α_y in the Taylor rule.

9.2.3 Long-Term Consequences

Another line of inquiry is the long-term economic consequences of IOCS. One implication that can be taken from IOCS is that it is consistent with greater long–term economic prosperity. At the broad macro level, we know that inflation instability and information coordination failure result in a diversion of resources that adversely affects the stock of aggregate wealth and economic growth.[11] The standard

---

[11] There are many studies that focus on this issue. See, for example, Leijonhufvud (1977), Stockman (1981), Jarrett and Selody (1982), Kormendi and Meguire (1985), Grier and Tullock (1989), DeGregorio (1992, 1993), Fischer (1993, 1996), Smyth (1994), Chari et al. (1995), Jones and Manuelli (1995), Ramey and Ramey (1995), and Bange et al. (1997)).

We note, however, there is disagreement on the precise long-term relation between inflation and economic growth. This issue may also be split along policymaker and academic lines. Consider the disagreement between Alan Greenspan and Laurence Meyer. Greenspan believes that "there is a strong link between price stability and higher productivity growth – so much so that the achievement of price stability would also raise the economy's maximum sustainable growth" (Meyer 2004: 213). Meyer, on the other hand, does not "believe that the Fed's effort to reduce inflation was somehow responsible for the wave of innovation that propelled the acceleration of productivity in the second half of the 1990s"(Meyer 2004: 214).

argument rests on the uncertainty that inflation brings to future real wages and real returns on nominally denominated assets. Inflation invariably reduces future consumption.

Predictably, the public attempts to avoid these reductions in its future consumption. As inflation rises, more resources are allocated to unproductive uses, such as hedging and speculation. Capital inputs in the form of real money balances are held at lower levels, and relative price distortions and uncertainty increase. As a result, the growth of output declines, and aggregate wealth depreciates more rapidly. The issue, then, is whether countries that consistently have IOCS outcomes have superior long–term economic performance.

9.3 Final Thoughts

A final issue is exploring how the various economic situations influence policy effectiveness. This focus on the overall economic environment is necessary to determine how much of the policy-IOCS linkage has been caused by fortuitous economic macroeconomic circumstances and how much by policy acumen.

In a related matter, much work needs to be done on finding out how aggressive inflation-stabilizing policy interacts when the size of the demand or supply shock changes. In general, the robustness of policy recommendations will ultimately depend on the quality of the economic understanding and the model that incorporates such knowledge. At this point, the relation between policy and IOCS would also benefit from a thorough examination of the stage in the business cycle at which this relation holds best and the feasible range of policy actions that best coordinate information and sustain IOCS.

In the end, what we have attempted to do is focus attention on the best role that a policymaker can provide – that of information coordinator. In doing so, we contend this particular policy role provides greater assurance that economic distress that results from self-inflicted – and preventable – policy errors can be avoided. The macroeconomic experiences of many countries testify to the variation in the way in which some countries make policy errors. Ultimately, improvements on our model will help us understand why some countries correct their policy mistakes, but others have yet to succeed.

References

Abel, A. B., 1997, "Comment," in C. D. Romer and D. H. Romer (eds.) *Reducing Inflation: Motivation and Strategy*, University of Chicago Press, Chicago.

Ahearne, A., J. Gagnon, J. Haltmaier, and S. Kamin, 2002, "Preventing Deflation: Lessons from Japan's Experience in the 1990s," *Federal Reserve Board International Finance Discussion Paper*, 729.

Akerlof, G., 1970, "The Market for 'Lemons': Quality Uncertainty and the Market Mechanism," *Quarterly Journal of Economics*, 84, 488–500.

Akerlof, G., W. T. Dickens, and G. Perry, 1996, "The Macroeconomics of Low Inflation," *Brookings Papers on Economic Activity*, 1, 1–59.

Akerlof, G., W. T. Dickens, and G. Perry, 2000, "Near-Rational Wage and Price Setting and the Long-Run Phillips Curve," *Brookings Papers on Economic Activity*, 1, 1–44.

Albanesi, S., V. V. Chari, and L. J. Christiano, 2003, "How Severe Is the Time-Inconsistency Problem in Monetary Policy?," *Federal Reserve Bank of Minneapolis Quarterly Review*, Summer, 17–33.

References

Alchian, A., and B. Klein, 1973, "On a Correct Measure of Inflation," *Journal of Money, Credit, and Banking,* 5, 173–81.

Alesina, A., and H. Rosenthal, 1995, *Partisan Politics, Divided Government, and the Economy,* Cambridge University Press, New York.

Alogoskoufis, G., 1992, "Monetary Accommodation, Exchange Rate Regimes and Inflation Persistence," *Economic Journal,* 102, 461–80.

Alogoskoufis, G., and R. Smith, 1991, "The Phillips Curve, the Persistence of Inflation, and the Lucas Critique," *American Economic Review,* 81, 1254–75.

Andersen, P., and D. Gruen, 1995, "Macroeconomic Policies and Growth," *Reserve Bank of Australia Research Discussion Paper,* 9507.

Andrews, D. W. K, 1993, "Tests for Parameter Instability and Structural Change with Unknown Change Point," *Econometrica,* 61, 821–56.

Arestis, P., and K. Mouratidis, 2002, "Is There a Trade-Off between Inflation Variability and Output-Gap Variability in the EMU Countries?," Typescript, Bard College and National Institute of Economic and Social Research.

Ball, L., 1994, "What Determines the Sacrifice Ratio?," in N. G. Mankiw (ed.), *Monetary Policy,* University of Chicago Press.

Ball, L., 1999, "Policy Rules for Open Economies," in J. B. Taylor (ed.), *Monetary Policy Rules,* University of Chicago Press.

Ball, L., and N. G. Mankiw, 1995, "Relative Price Changes as Aggregate Supply Shocks," *Quarterly Journal of Economics,* 110, 161–93.

Ball, L., and D. Romer, 2003, "Inflation and the Informativeness of Prices," *The Journal of Money, Credit, and Banking,* 35, 177–96.

Bange, M., W. Bernhard, J. Granato, and L. Jones, 1997, "The Effect of Inflation on the Natural Rate of Output: Experimental Evidence," *Applied Economics,* 29, 1191–9.

Barbeau, E. J., 1989, *Polynomials,* Springer-Verlag, New York.

References

Barro, R., 1997, *The Determinants of Economic Growth*, MIT Press, Cambridge, MA.

Barro, R., and D. Gordon, 1983a, "Rules, Discretion and Reputation in a Model of Monetary Policy," *Journal of Monetary Economics*, 12, 101–21.

Barro, R., and D. Gordon, 1983b, "A Positive Theory of Monetary Policy in a Natural Rate Model," *Journal of Political Economy*, 91, 589–609.

Barro, R., and H. Grossman, 1976, *Money, Employment, and Inflation*, Cambridge University Press, New York.

Baxter, M. 1985, "The Role of Expectations in Stabilization Policy," *Journal of Monetary Economics*, 15, 343–62.

Bernanke, B. S., 2004, "Fedspeak," presented at the American Economic Association Annual Meeting, San Diego, CA.

Bernanke, B. S., and A. Blinder, 1992, "The Federal Funds Rate and the Channels of Monetary Transmission," *American Economic Review*, 82, 901–21.

Bernanke, B. S., T. Laubach, F. S. Mishkin, and A. S. Posen, 1999, *Inflation Targeting: Lessons from the International Experience*, Princeton University Press, Princeton, NJ.

Bernanke, B. S., and I. Mihov, 1998a, "The Liquidity Effect and Long-Run Neutrality," *Carnegie-Rochester Series on Public Policy*, 49, 149–94.

Bernanke, B. S., and I. Mihov, 1998b, "Measuring Monetary Policy," *Quarterly Journal of Economics*, 113, 869–902.

Bernanke, B. S., and M. Woodford, 1997, "Inflation Forecasts and Monetary Policy," *Journal of Money, Credit, and Banking*, 29, 653–84.

Bernhard, W., 2002, *Banking on Reform: Political Parties and Central Bank Independence in the Industrial Democracies*, University of Michigan Press, Ann Arbor.

References

Blanchard, O., and J. Simon, 2001, "The Long and Large Decline in U.S. Output Volatility," *Brookings Papers on Economic Activity*, 1, 135–74.

Bleaney, M., 1999, "Price and Monetary Dynamics under Alternative Exchange Rate Regimes," *IMF Working Paper*, 99/67.

Bleaney, M., 2001, "Exchange Rate Regimes and Inflation Persistence," *IMF Staff Papers*, 47, 3.

Blinder, A., 1982, "The Anatomy of Double-Digit Inflation," in R. E. Hall (ed.), *Inflation: Causes and Effects*, University of Chicago Press, Chicago.

Blinder, A., 1998, *Central Banking in Theory and Practice*, MIT Press, Cambridge, MA.

Bomfim, A. N., 1997, "The Equilibrium Fed Funds Rate and the Indicator Properties of Term-Structure Spreads," *Economic Inquiry*, 35, 830–46.

Bosworth, B., 1989, "Institutional Change and the Efficacy of Monetary Policy," *Brookings Papers on Economic Activity*, 1, 77–110.

Brainard, W., 1967, "Uncertainty and the Effectiveness of Policy," *American Economic Review*, 57, 411–25.

Bray, M., 1982, "Learning, Estimation, and the Stability of Rational Expectations," *Journal of Economic Theory*, 26, 318–39.

Bray, M., and N. E. Savin, 1986, "Rational Expectations, Equilibria, Learning, and Model Specification," *Econometrica*, 54, 1129–60.

Breeden, D., 1979, "An Intertemporal Asset Pricing Model with Stochastic Consumption and Investment Opportunities," *Journal of Financial Economics*, 7, 265–96.

Brunner, K., and A. H. Meltzer, 1969, "The Nature of the Problem," in *Targets and Indicators of Monetary Policy*, ed. K. Brunner, Chandler Publishing Company, San Francisco.

References

Brunner, K., A. Cukierman, and A. H. Meltzer, 1980, "Stagfla-tion, Persistent Unemployment and the Permanence of Eco-nomic Shocks," *Journal of Monetary Economics*, 6, 467–92.

Brunner, K., A. Cukierman, and A. H. Meltzer, 1983, "Money and Economic Activity, Inventories and Business Cycles," *Journal of Monetary Economics*, 11, 281–319.

Bruno, M., and W. Easterly, 1998, "Inflation Crises and Long-Run Growth," *Journal of Monetary Economics*, 41, 3–26.

Bryant, R., P. Hooper, and C. Mann (eds.), 1993, *Evaluating Pol-icy Regimes: New Research in Empirical Macroeconomics*, Brookings Institution, Washington, DC.

Bullard, J., 1998, "Trading Trade-Offs?,"*National Economic Trends*, Federal Reserve Bank of St. Louis.

Bullard, J., and K. Mitra, 2001, "Determinacy, Learnability and Monetary Policy Inertia," Working Paper: www.stls.frb.org/research/econ/bullard.

Bullard, J., and K. Mitra, 2002, "Learning about Monetary Policy Rules," *Journal of Monetary Economics*, 49, 1105–29.

Bulman, T., and J. Simon, 2003, "Productivity and Inflation," *Reserve Bank of Australia Research Discussion Paper*, 2003–10.

Burdekin, R. C. K., and P. L. Siklos, 1999, "Exchange Rate Regimes and Shifts in Inflation Persistence: Does Nothing Else Matter?," *Journal of Money, Credit, and Banking*, 31, 235–47.

Burns, A. F., and W. C. Mitchell, 1946, *Measuring Business Cycles*, National Bureau of Economic Research, New York.

Canterbery, R., 1968, *Economics on a New Frontier*, Wadsworth, Belmont, UK.

Carpenter, S. B., 2004, "Transparency and Monetary Policy: What Does the Academic Literature Tell Policymakers?," *Federal Reserve Board Finance and Economics Discussion Series*, 2004–35.

References

Cecchetti, S., and M. Ehrmann. 1999/2002, "Does Inflation Targeting Increase Output Volatility? An International Comparison of Policymakers' Preferences and Outcomes," in N. Loayza and K. Schmidt-Hebbel (eds.), *Monetary Policy: Rules and Transmission Mechanisms*, Central Bank of Chile and NBER Working Paper No. 7426, Santiago.

Chappell, H. W., R. R. McGregor, and T. A. Verymilyea, 2005, *Committee Decisions on Monetary Policy: Evidence from Historical Records of the Federal Reserve Open Market Committee*, MIT Press, Cambridge, MA.

Chari, V. V., L. E. Jones, and R. Manuelli, 1995, "The Growth Effects of Monetary Policy," *Federal Reserve Bank of Minneapolis Quarterly Review*, Fall, 18–32.

Chow, G., 1960, "Tests of Equality between Sets of Coefficients in Two Linear Regressions," *Econometrica* 28, 591–605.

Chung, H., 1990, *Did Policymakers Really Believe in the Phillips Curve?, An Econometric Test*, University of Minnesota, Ph.D. thesis.

Clarida, R., J. Gali, and M. Gertler, 1999, "The Science of Monetary Policy: A New Keynesian Perspective," *Journal of Economic Perspectives*, 37, 1661–707.

Clarida, R., J. Gali, and M. Gertler, 2000, "Monetary Policy Rules and Macroeconomic Stability: Evidence and Some Theory," *Quarterly Journal of Economics*, 115, 147–80.

Cogley, T., and T. J. Sargent, 2001, "Evolving Post World War II U.S. Inflation Dynamics," *NBER Macroeconomics Annual*, 16, 331–73.

Cogley, T., and T. J. Sargent, 2002, "Drifts and Volatilities: Monetary Policies and Outcomes in the Post WWII U.S.," Typescript, Arizona State University and New York University.

Collard, F., and H. Dellas, 2004, "The Great Inflation of the 1970s," *Federal Reserve Board International Finance Discussion Paper*, 2004–799.

References

Cooper, R. W., 1999, *Coordination Games: Complimentarities and Macroeconomics*, Cambridge University Press, New York.

Cooper, R. W., and A. John, 1988, "Coordinating Coordination Failures in Keynesian Models," *Quarterly Journal of Economics*, 103, 441–63.

Cukierman, A., 1986, "Central Bank Behavior and Credibility: Some Recent Theoretical Developments," *Review: Federal Reserve Bank of St. Louis*, May, 5–17.

Cukierman, A., and A. H. Meltzer, 1986, "A Theory of Ambiguity, Credibility, and Inflation under Discretion and Asymmetric information," *Econometrica*, 54, 1099–128.

Cukierman, A., and P. Wachtel, 1979, "Differential Inflationary Expectations and the Variability of the Rate of Inflation: Theory and Evidence," *American Economic Review*, 69, 595–609.

Debelle, G., and S. Fischer, 1994, "How Independent Should a Central Bank Be?," in J. C. Fuhrer (ed.), *Goals, Guidelines, and Constraints Facing Policymakers*, Federal Reserve Bank of Boston.

DeGregorio, J., 1992, "The Effects of Inflation on Economic Growth: Lessons from Latin America," *European Economic Review*, 36, 417–25.

DeGregorio, J., 1993, "Inflation, Taxation, and Long-Run Growth," *Journal of Monetary Economics*, 31, 271–98.

DeLong, J. B., 1997, "America's Peacetime Inflation: The 1970s," in C. D. Romer and D. H. Romer (eds.), *Reducing Inflation: Motivation and Strategy*, University of Chicago Press.

Dennis, R., 2003, "The Policy Preferences of the US Federal Reserve," Typescript, Federal Reserve Bank of San Francisco.

Diebold, F. X., and G. D. Rudebusch, 1999, *Business Cycles*, Princeton University Press, Princeton, NJ.

Dittmar, R., W. T. Gavin, and F. E. Kydland, 1999, "The Inflation-Output Variability Trade-Off and Price-Level Targets," *Review: Federal Reserve Bank of St. Louis* January/February, 23–32.

References

Drazen, A., 2000, *Political Economy in Macroeconomics*, Princeton University Press, Princeton, NJ.

Driscoll, J. C., and S. Holden, 2003, "Coordination, Fair Treatment and Inflation Persistence," *Federal Reserve Board Finance and Economics Discussion Series*, 2003–34.

Driscoll, J. C., and H. Ito, 2003, "Sticky Prices, Coordination and Enforcement," *Federal Reserve Board Finance and Economics Discussion Series*, 2003–30.

Erceg, C. J., D. W. Henderson, and A. T. Levin, 1998, "Trade-Offs between Inflation and Output-Gap Variances in an Optimizing Agent Model," *Federal Reserve Board International Finance Discussion Paper*, 1998–627.

Estrella, A., and J. C. Fuhrer, 2003, "Monetary Policy Shifts and the Stability of Monetary Policy Models," *The Review of Economics and Statistics*, 85, 94–104.

Evans, G. W., 1985, "Expectational Stability and the Multiple Equilibrium Problem in Linear Rational Expectations Models," *The Quarterly Journal of Economics*, 100, 1217–33.

Evans, G. W., 1989, "The Fragility of Sunspots and Bubbles," *Journal of Monetary Economics*, 23, 297–313.

Evans, G. W., and R. Guesnerie (eds.), 2003, "Special Issue on Coordination in Dynamic Expectations Models: Learning and Sunspots," in W. A. Barnett (ed.), *Macroeconomic Dynamics*, 7.

Evans, G. W., and S. Honkapohja, 1995, "Adaptive Learning and Expectational Stability: An Introduction," in A. Kirman and M. Salmon (eds.), *Learning and Rationality in Economics*, Basil Blackwell, Oxford.

Evans, G., and S. Honkapohja, 2001, *Learning and Expectations in Macroeconomics*, Princeton University Press, Princeton, NJ.

Faust, J., and D. W. Henderson, 2004, "Is Inflation Targeting Best-Practice?," *Federal Reserve Board International Finance Discussion Paper*, 2004–807.

References

Federal Reserve Bank of Kansas City, 1996, *Achieving Price Stability*.

Federal Reserve Bank of Kansas City, 1999, *New Challenges for Monetary Policy*.

Federal Reserve Bank of Kansas City, 2002, *Rethinking Stabilization Policy*.

Federal Reserve Bank of Kansas City, 2003, *Monetary Policy and Uncertainty: Adapting to a Changing Economy*.

Feldstein, M., 1997, "The Costs and Benefits of Going from Low Inflation to Price Stability," in C. D. Romer and D. H. Romer (ed.), *Reducing Inflation: Motivation and Strategy*, University of Chicago Press.

Fisher, I., 1926/1973, "A Statistical Relation between Unemployment and Price Changes," *International Labor Review*, 13, 785–92. Reprinted in *Journal of Political Economy*, 81, 496–502.

Fisher, I., 1933, "Debt-Deflation Theory of Great Depressions," *Econometrica*, 1, 357–77.

Fischer, S. 1977, "Long-Term Contracts, Rational Expectations, and the Optimal Money Supply Rule," *Journal of Political Economy*, 85, 191–205.

Fischer, S. (ed.), 1980, *Rational Expectations and Economic Policy*, University of Chicago Press.

Fischer, S., 1993, "The Role of Macroeconomic Factors in Growth," *Journal of Monetary Economics*, 32, 485–512.

Fischer, S., 1994, "Modern Central Banking," in F. Capie, S. Fischer, C. Goodhart, and B. Schnadt (eds.), *The Future of Central Banking: The Tercernary Symposium of The Bank of England*, Cambridge University Press, New York.

Fischer, S., 1996, "Why Are Central Banks Pursuing Long-Run Price Stability?," in *Achieving Price Stability*, Federal Reserve Bank of Kansas City.

Franzese, R. J., Jr., 2002, *Macroeconomic Policies of Developed Democracies*, Cambridge University Press, New York.

References

Freeman, J. R., 2002, "Competing Commitments: Technocracy and Democracy in the Design of Monetary Institutions," *International Organization*, 56, 889–910.

Friedman, M., 1948, "A Monetary and Fiscal Framework for Economic Stability," *American Economic Review*, 38, 245–64.

Friedman, M., 1957, *A Theory of the Consumption Function*, Princeton University Press, Princeton, NJ.

Friedman, M., 1960, *A Program for Monetary Stability*, Fordham University Press, New York.

Friedman, M., 1963, *Inflation: Causes and Consequences*, Asia Publishing House, New York.

Friedman, M., 1968, "The Role of Monetary Policy," *American Economic Review*, 58, 1–17.

Friedman, M., 1969, "Factors Affecting the Level of Interest Rates," presented at the Conference on Savings and Residential Financings sponsored by the United States Savings and Loan League, Chicago.

Friedman, M., 1977, "Nobel Lecture: Inflation and Unemployment," *Journal of Political Economy*, 85, 451–72.

Friedman, M., and A. J. Schwartz, 1963, *A Monetary History of the United States, 1867–1960*, Princeton University Press, Princeton, NJ.

Friedman, M., and A. J. Schwartz, 1970, *Monetary Statistics of the United States*, NBER, New York.

Fuhrer, J. C. (ed.), 1994, *Goals, Guidelines, and Constraints Facing Policymakers*, Federal Reserve Bank of Boston.

Fuhrer, J. C., 1995, "The Persistence of Inflation and the Cost of Disinflation," *New England Economic Review: Federal Reserve Bank of Boston*, January/February, 3–16.

Fuhrer, J. C., and G. Moore, 1995a, "Inflation Persistence," *Quarterly Journal of Economics*, 110, 127–59.

References

Fuhrer, J. C., and G. Moore, 1995b, "Monetary Policy Trade-Offs and the Correlation between Nominal Interest Rates and Real Output," *American Economic Review*, 85, 219–39.

Fuhrer, J. C., and S. Schuh. (eds.), 1998, *Beyond Shocks: What Causes Business Cycles?*, Federal Reserve Bank of Boston.

Gavin, W. T., and R. J. Mandal, 2001, "Forecasting Inflation and Growth: Do Private Forecasts Match Those of Policymakers?," *Review: Federal Reserve Bank of St. Louis*, May/June, 11–20.

Goldfeld, S. M., and R. E. Quandt, 1973, "The Estimation of Structural Shifts by Switching Regressions," *Annals of Economic and Social Measurement*, 2, 475–85.

Gomme, P., 1998, "Canada's Money Targeting Experiment," *Economic Commentary, Federal Reserve Bank of Cleveland*, February.

Goodfriend, M., 1993, "Interest Rate Policy and the Inflation Scare Problem: 1979–1992," *Economic Quarterly. Richmond: Federal Reserve Bank of Richmond*, 79, 1–24.

Goodfriend, M., 1995, "Acquiring and Maintaining Credibility for Low Inflation: The U.S. Experience," in L. Leiderman and L. E. O. Svensson (eds.), *Inflation Targets*, Center for Economic Policy Research, London.

Goodhart, C. A. E., and J. Viñals, 1994, "Strategy and Tactics of Monetary Policy: Examples from Europe and the Antipodes," in J. C. Fuhrer (ed.), *Goals, Guidelines, and Constraints Facing Policymakers*, Federal Reserve Bank of Boston.

Granato, J., 1996, "The Effect of Policymaker Reputation and Credibility on Public Expectations: An Application to Macroeconomic Policy Changes," *Journal of Theoretical Politics*, 8, 549–70.

Granato, J., D. C. Diller, and D. J. Peterson, 2002, "Chief Economist," in M. Nelson (ed.), *Guide to the Presidency*, 3d ed., vol. 1, Congressional Quarterly Press, Washington, DC.

References

Granato, J., M. Lo, and S. M. C. Wong, 2006, "Testing Monetary Policy Intentions in Open Economies," *Southern Economic Journal*, 72, 225–41.

Granato, J., and S. M. C. Wong, 2005, "The Boomerang Effect: Learning from the Expectations of Others," Typescript, University of Southern Mississippi and the National Science Foundation (NSF), and the University of Texas at Austin.

Gray, J., 1976, "Wage Indexation: A Macroeconomic Approach," *Journal of Monetary Economics*, 2, 221–35.

Gray, J., 1978, "On Indexation and Contract Length," *Journal of Political Economy*, 86, 1–18.

Greenspan, A., 2004, "Risk and Uncertainty in Monetary Policy," presented at the American Economic Association Annual Meeting, San Diego, CA.

Greider, W., 1987, *Secrets of the Temple*, Simon and Schuster, New York.

Grier, K. B., and G. Tullock, 1989, "An Empirical Analysis of Cross-Sectional Economic Growth," *Journal of Monetary Economics*, 24, 259–76.

Groshen, E. L., and M. E. Schweitzer, 1996, "The Effects of Inflation on Wage Adjustments in Firm-Level Data: Grease or Sand?," *Staff Report, Federal Reserve Bank of New York*, no. 9.

Hansen, L. P., and J. J. Heckman, 1996, "The Empirical Foundations of Calibration," *The Journal of Economic Perspectives*, 10, 87–104.

Havrilesky, T., 1993, *The Pressures on Monetary Policy*. Kluwer Academic Publishers, Norwell, MA.

Hayek, F. A., 1945, "The Use of Knowledge in Society," *American Economic Review*, 35, 519–30.

Hess, G. D., and C. S. Morris, 1996, "The Long-Run Costs of Moderate Inflation," *Economic Review: Federal Reserve Bank of Kansas City*, Second Quarter, 71–88.

References

Hetzel, R. L., 2000, "The Taylor Rule: Is It a Useful Guide to Understanding Monetary Policy?," *Economic Quarterly: Federal Reserve Bank of Richmond*, Spring, 1–33.

Hinkley, D. V., 1971, "Inference in Two-Phase Regression," *Journal of the American Statistical Association*, 66, 736–43.

Huizinga, J., and F. S. Mishkin, 1986, "Monetary Policy Regime Shifts and the Unusual Behavior of Real Interest Rates," in K. Brunner and A. H. Meltzer (eds.), *The National Bureau Method, International Capital Mobility and Other Essays*, North Holland, Amsterdam.

International Monetary Fund Task Force, 2003, *Deflation: Determinants, Risks, and Policy Options–Findings of an Interdepartmental Task Force*.

Ireland, P. N., 1999, "Does the Time-Consistency Problem Explain the Behavior of Inflation in the United States?," *Journal of Monetary Economics*, 44, 279–91.

Iversen, T., 1999, *Contested Economic Institutions: The Politics of Macroeconomics and Wage Bargaining in Advanced Democracies*, Cambridge University Press, New York.

Jarrett, J. P., and J. Selody, 1982, "The Productivity-Inflation Nexus in Canada, 1963–1979," *Review of Economics and Statistics*, 64, 361–7.

Johnson, K., D. Small, and R. Tryon, 1999, "Monetary Policy and Price Stability," *Federal Reserve Board International Finance Discussion Paper*, 1999–641.

Jones, L. E., and R. E. Manuelli, 1995, "Growth and the Effects of Inflation," *Journal of Economic Dynamics and Control*, 19, 1405–28.

Judson, R., and A. Orphanides, 1996, "Inflation, Volatility, and Growth," *Federal Reserve Board Finance and Economics Discussion Series*, 1996–16.

Kahn, J. A., M. M. McConnell, and G. Perez-Quiros, 2001, "Inventories and the Information Revolution: Implications for

References

Output Volatility," *Federal Reserve Bank of New York Working Paper.*

Kahn, J. A., M. M. McConnell, and G. Perez-Quiros, 2002, "On the Causes of the Increased Stability of the U. S. Economy," *Economic Policy Review: Federal Reserve Bank of New York,* May, 183–202.

Kandel, E., and B.-Z. Zilberfarb, 1999, "Differential Interpretation of Information in Inflation Forecasts," *The Review of Economics and Statistics,* 81, 217–26.

Katzner, D., 1989, *The Walrasian Vision of the Microeconomy: An Elementary Exposition of the Structure of Modern General Equilibrium Theory,* University of Michigan Press, Ann Arbor.

Kettl, D., 1986, *Leadership at the Fed,* Yale University Press, New Haven, CT.

Keynes, J. M., 1936, *The General Theory of Employment, Interest, and Money,* Macmillan, London.

Kim, C., and C. R. Nelson, 1999, "Has the U.S. Economy Become More Stable? A Bayesian Approach Based on a Markov-Switching Model of the Business Cycle," *The Review of Economics and Statistics,* 81, 608–16.

Kimura, T., and T. Kurozumi, 2003, "Optimal Monetary Policy in a Micro-Founded Model with Parameter Uncertainty," *Federal Reserve Board Finance and Economics Discussion Series,* 2003–67.

Kohn, D. L., and B. P. Sack, 2003, "Central Bank Talk: Does It Matter and Why?," *Federal Reserve Board Finance and Economics Discussion Series,* 2003–55.

Kormendi, R. C., and P. G. Meguire, 1985, "Macroeconomic Determinants of Growth: Cross-Country Evidence," *Journal of Monetary Economics,* 16, 141–63.

Kozicki, S., 1999, "How Useful Are Taylor Rules for Monetary Policy?," *Economic Review: Federal Reserve Bank of Kansas City,* Second Quarter, 5–33.

References

Kuttner, K. N., and A. S. Posen, 1999, "Does Talk Matter After All? Inflation Targeting and Central Bank Behavior," *Staff Report, Federal Reserve Bank of New York*, no. 88.

Kydland, F. E., and E. C. Prescott, 1977, "Rules rather than Discretion: The Inconsistency of Optimal Plans," *Journal of Political Economy*, 85, 473–91.

Kydland, F. E., and E. C. Prescott, 1982, "Time to Build and Aggregate Fluctuations," *Econometrica*, 50, 1345–70.

Kydland, F. E., and E. C. Prescott, 1996, "The Computational Experiment: An Econometric Tool," *The Journal of Economic Perspectives*, 10, 69–85.

Labhard, V., 2003, "What Explains Changes in Postwar Output Volatility: Shocks or Propagation Mechanisms?," Typescript, International Economic Analysis Division, Bank of England.

Lane, P. R., 1997, "Inflation in Open Economies," *Journal of International Economics*, 42, 327–47.

Lansing, K. J., 2001, "Learning about a Shift in Trend Output: Implications for Monetary Policy and Inflation," Typescript, Federal Reserve Bank of San Francisco.

Leiderman, L., and L. E. O. Svensson (eds.), 1995, *Inflation Targets*, Center for Economic Policy Research, London.

Leijonhufvud, A., 1968, *On Keynesian Economics and the Economics of Keynes*, Oxford University Press, Oxford.

Leijonhufvud, A., 1977, "Costs and Consequences of Inflation," in G. C. Harcourt (ed.), *Microeconomic Foundations of Macroeconomics*, Westview Press, Boulder, CO.

Levin, A., V. Wieland, and J. Williams, 1999, "Robustness of Simple Monetary Policy Rules under Model Uncertainty," in J. B. Taylor (ed.), *Monetary Policy Rules*, University of Chicago Press.

Long, J. B., and C. I. Plosser, 1983, "Real Business Cycles," *Journal of Political Economy*, 91, 39–69.

References

Lucas, R. E., Jr., 1972, "Expectations and the Neutrality of Money," *Journal of Economic Theory*, 4, 103–24.

Lucas, R. E., Jr., 1973, "Some International Evidence on Output-Inflation Trade-Offs," *American Economic Review*, 63, 326–34.

Lucas, R. E., Jr., 1976, "Econometric Policy Evaluation: A Critique," *Carnegie-Rochester Conference on Public Policy*, 1, 19–46.

Lucas, R. E., Jr., 1980, "Rules, Discretion, and the Role of the Economic Advisor," in S. Fischer (ed.), *Rational Expectations and Economic Policy*, University of Chicago Press.

Lucas, R. E., Jr., 2003, "Macroeconomic Priorities," *American Economic Review*, 93, 1–14.

Magnus, J. R., and H. Neudecker, 1999, *Matrix Differential Calculus with Applications in Statistics and Econometrics*, John Wiley & Sons, New York.

Mankiw, N. G., 2001, "U.S. Monetary Policy in the 1990s," *NBER Working Paper*, 8471.

Mankiw, N. G., and R. Reis, 2002, "Sticky Information versus Sticky Prices: A Proposal to Replace the New Keynesian Phillips Curve," *Quarterly Journal of Economics*, 117, 1295–1328.

Mankiw, N. G., and D. Romer (eds.), 1991, *New Keynesian Economics*, MIT Press, Cambridge, MA.

Marcet, A., and T. J. Sargent, 1989a, "Convergence of Least-Squares Learning in Environments with Hidden State Variables and Private Information," *Journal of Political Economy*, 97, 1306–22.

Marcet, A., and T. J. Sargent, 1989b, "Convergence of Least-Squares Learning Mechanisms in Self-Referential Linear Stochastic Models," *Journal of Economic Theory*, 48, 337–68.

Martin, B., and R. Rowthorn, 2004, "Will Stability Last?," Research Paper, *UBS Global Asset Management*.

References

Mayer, T., 1999, *Monetary Policy and the Great Inflation in the United States: The Federal Reserve and the Failure of Macroeconomic Policy, 1965–1979*, Edward Elgar, Cheltenham, UK.

McCallum, B. T., 1981, "Price Level Determinacy with an Interest Rate Policy Rule and Rational Expectations," *Journal of Monetary Economics*, 8, 319–29.

McCallum, B. T., 1983, "On Nonuniqueness in Linear Rational Expectations Models: An Attempt at Perspective," *The Journal of Monetary Economics*, 11, 134–68.

McCallum, B. T., 1989, *Monetary Economics: Theory and Policy*, Macmillan, New York.

McCallum, B. T., 1994, "Identification of Inflation-Unemployment Tradeoffs in the 1970s: A Comment," *Carnegie-Rochester Conference on Public Policy* 41, 231–41.

McCallum, B. T., 1999, "Role of the Minimal State Variable Criterion in Rational Expectations Models," *International Tax and Public Finance*, 6, 621–39.

McCallum, B. T., 2001a, "Monetary Policy Analysis in Models without Money," *Review: Federal Reserve Bank of St. Louis* July/August, 145–60.

McCallum, B. T., 2001b, "Should Monetary Policy Respond Strongly to Output Gaps?," *American Economic Review*, 91, 258–62.

McCallum, B. T., 2002a, "Inflation Targeting and the Liquidity Trap," in N. Loayza and R. Soto (eds.), *Ten Years of Inflation Targeting: Design, Performance, Challenges*, Central Bank of Chile, Santiago, Chile.

McCallum, B. T., 2002b, "The Unique Minimum State Variable RE Solution is E-Stable in All Well Formulated Linear Models," Typescript, Carnegie Mellon and NBER.

References

McCallum, B. T., 2003, "Multiple-Solution Indeterminacies in Monetary Policy Analysis," *Journal of Monetary Economics*, 50, 1153–75.

McCallum, B. T., and E. Nelson, 1999, "An Optimizing IS-LM Specification for Monetary Policy and Business Cycle Analysis," *Journal of Money, Credit, and Banking*, 31, 296–316.

McConnell, M. M., and G. Perez-Quiros, 2000, "Output Fluctuations in the United States: What has Changed Since the Early 1980s?," *American Economic Review*, 90, 1464–76.

McGee, V. E., and W. T. Carlton, 1970, "Piecewise Regression," *Journal of the American Statistical Association*, 65, 1109–24.

Mehra, Y. P., 2002, "The Taylor Principle, Interest Rate Smoothing and Fed Policy in the 1970s and 1980s," *Federal Reserve Bank of Richmond Working Paper*, 02–03.

Melton, W. C., 1985, *Inside the Fed: Making Monetary Policy*, Dow Jones-Irwin, Homewood, IL.

Meltzer, A. H., 1987, "Limits of Short-Run Stabilization Policy: Presidential Address to the Western Economic Association," *Economic Inquiry*, 25, 1–14.

Meltzer, A. H., 2003, *A History of the Federal Reserve*, Vol. 1, *1913–1951*, University of Chicago Press.

Meyer, L. H., 2004, *A Term at the Fed: An Insider's View*, Harper-Collins, New York.

Mishkin, F., 1999, "Comment," in J. B. Taylor (ed.), *Monetary Policy Rules*, University of Chicago Press.

Mitchell, W. C., 1913, *Business Cycles*, University of California Press, Berkeley.

Mitchell, W. C., 1951, *What Happens during Business Cycles*, National Bureau of Economic Research, New York.

Morris, I., 2000, *Congress, the President, and the Federal Reserve: The Politics of American Monetary Policy-Making*, University of Michigan Press, Ann Arbor.

References

Muth, J., 1961, "Rational Expectations and the Theory of Price Movements," *Econometrica*, 29, 315–33.

Nelson, E., 2004, "The Great Inflation of the Seventies: What Really Happened?," *Federal Reserve Bank of St. Louis Working Paper*, 2004–001.

Obstfeld, M., 1995, "International Currency Experience: New Lessons and Lessons Relearned," *Brookings Papers on Economic Activity*, 1, 119–220.

Orphanides, A., 2002, "Monetary Policy Rules and the Great Inflation," *American Economic Review*, 92, 115–20.

Orphanides, A., 2003, "Historical Monetary Policy Analysis and the Taylor Rule," *Federal Reserve Board Finance and Economics Discussion Series*, 2003–36.

Orphanides, A., 2004, "Monetary Policy in Deflation: The Liquidity Trap in History and Practice," *Federal Reserve Board Finance and Economics Discussion Series*, 2004–01.

Orphanides, A., and J. Williams, 2003a, "Imperfect Knowledge, Inflation Expectations, and Monetary Policy," *NBER Working Paper* 9884.

Orphanides, A., and J. Williams, 2003b, "Inflation Scares and Forecast-Based Monetary Policy," *Federal Reserve Board Finance and Economics Discussion Series*, 2003–41.

Orphanides, A., and J. Williams, 2004, "The Decline of Activist Stabilization Policy: Natural Rate Misperceptions, Learning and Expectations," *Federal Reserve Board International Finance Discussion Paper*, 2004–804.

Owyang, M. T., 2001, "Persistence, Excess Volatility, and Volatility Clusters in Inflation," *Review: Federal Reserve Bank of St. Louis* November/December, 41–51.

Owyang, M., and G. Ramey, 2002, "Regime Switching and Monetary Policy Measurement," Typescript, Federal Reserve Bank of St. Louis and University of California, San Diego.

References

Parks, R., 1978, "Inflation and Relative Price Variability," *Journal of Political Economy*, 86, 79–95.

Persson, T., and G. Tabellini, 2000, *Political Economics: Explaining Economic Policy*. MIT Press, Cambridge, MA.

Phelps, E. S., 1968, "Money-Wage Dynamics and Labor-Market Equilibrium," *Journal of Political Economy*, 76, 678–711.

Phillips, A. W., 1958, "The Relation between Unemployment and the Rate of Change in Money Wage Rates in the United Kingdom, 1861–1957," *Economica*, 25, 283–99.

Phillips, P. C. B., 1998, "Impulse Response and Forecast Error Variance Asymptotics in Nonstationary VARs," *Journal of Econometrics*, 83, 21–56.

Piehl, A. M., S. J. Cooper, A. A. Braga, and D. M. Kennedy, 1999, "Testing for Structural Breaks in the Evaluation of Programs," *NBER Working Paper* 7226.

Poole, W., 1970, "Optimal Choice of Monetary Policy Instruments in a Simple Stochastic Model," *Quarterly Journal of Economics*, 84, 197–216.

Quandt, R. E., 1958, "The Estimation of the Parameters of a Linear Regression System Obeying Two Separate Regimes," *Journal of the American Statistical Association*, 53, 873–80.

Ramey, G., and V. Ramey, 1995, "Cross-Country Evidence on the Link between Volatility and Growth," *American Economic Review*, 85, 1138–51.

Romer, C. D., and D. H. Romer (eds.), 1997, *Reducing Inflation: Motivation and Strategy*, University of Chicago Press.

Romer, C. D., and D. H. Romer, 2002. "The Evolution of Economic Understanding and Postwar Stabilization Policy," in *Rethinking Stabilization Policy*, Federal Reserve Bank of Kansas City.

References

Romer, C. D., and D. H. Romer, 2004, "Choosing the Federal Reserve Chair: Lessons from History," *Journal of Economic Perspectives*, 18, 129–62.

Romer, D. H., 1993, "Openness and Inflation: Theory and Evidence," *Quarterly Journal of Economics*, 108, 869–903.

Romer, D. H., 2000, "Keynesian Macroeconomics without the LM Curve," *Journal of Economic Perspectives*, 14, 149–69.

Rotemberg, J., and M. Woodford, 1997, "An Optimization-Based Econometric Framework for the Evaluation of Monetary Policy," *NBER Macroeconomics Annual*, 13, 297–346.

Rotemberg, J., and M. Woodford, 1998, "An Optimization-Based Econometric Framework for the Evaluation of Monetary Policy: Expanded Version," *NBER Technical Working Paper* 233.

Rudd, J., and K. Whelan, 2003, "Can Rational Expectations Sticky-Price Models Explain Inflation Dynamics?," *Federal Reserve Board Finance and Economics Discussion Series*, 2003–46.

Rudebusch, G. D., and L. E. O. Svensson, 1999, "Policy Rules for Inflation Targeting," in J. B. Taylor (ed.), *Monetary Policy Rules*, University of Chicago Press.

Sack, B., and V. Wieland, 2000, "Interest Rate Smoothing and Optimal Monetary Policy: A Review of Recent Empirical Evidence," *Journal of Economics and Business*, 52, 205–28.

Samuelson, P., and R. Solow, 1960, "Analytical Aspects of Anti-Inflation Policy," *American Economic Review*, 50, 177–94.

Sarel, M., 1996, "Nonlinear Effects of Inflation on Economic Growth," *IMF Staff Papers*, 43, 199–215.

Sargent, T. J., 1987, *Macroeconomic Theory*, 2d ed., Academic Press, Orlando, FL.

Sargent, T. J., 1999, *The Conquest of American Inflation*, Princeton University Press, Princeton, NJ.

References

Sargent, T. J., 2002, "Commentary: The Evolution of Economic Understanding and Postwar Stabilization Policy," in *Rethinking Stabilization Policy*, Federal Reserve Bank of Kansas City.

Sargent, T. J., and U. Söderström, 2000, "The Conquest of American Inflation: A Summary," *Sveriges Riksbank Economic Review*, 3, 12–45.

Sargent, T. J., and N. Wallace, 1975, "Rational Expectations, the Optimal Monetary Instrument, and the Optimal Money Supply Rule," *Journal of Political Economy*, 83, 241–54.

Sheffrin, S. M., 1989, *The Making of Economic Policy*, Basil Blackwell, Cambridge, MA.

Siklos, P. L., 1999, "Inflation-Target Design: Changing Inflation Performance and Persistence in Industrial Countries," *Review: Federal Reserve Bank of St. Louis*, March/April, 47–58.

Siklos, P. L., 2002, *The Changing Face of Central Banking*, Cambridge University Press, New York.

Sims, C., 1988, "Projecting Policy Effects with Statistical Models," *Revista de Analisis Economico*, 3, 3–20.

Sims, C., 1996, "Macroeconomics and Methodology," *The Journal of Economic Perspectives*, 10, 105–20.

Sims, C., 1998, "The Role of Interest Rate Policy in the Generation and Propagation of Business Cycles: What Has Changed Since the '30s?," in J. C. Fuhrer and S. Schuh (eds.), *Beyond Shocks: What Causes Business Cycles?*, Federal Reserve Bank of Boston.

Smyth, D., 1994, "Inflation and Growth," *Journal of Macroeconomics* 16, 261–70.

Snyder, C., 1935, "The Problem of Monetary and Economic Stability," *Quarterly Journal of Economics*, 49, 173–205.

Söderström, U., and A. Vredin, 2000, "The Conquest of Inflation – An Introduction to Sargent's Analysis," *Sveriges Riksbank Economic Review*, 3, 5–11.

Sowell, T., 1980, *Knowledge and Decisions*, Basic Books, New York.

References

Stein, H., 1994, *Presidential Economics*, American Enterprise Institute, Washington, DC.

Stock, J. H., and M. W. Watson, 1988, "Testing for Common Trends," *Journal of the American Statistical Association*, 83, 1097–107.

Stock, J. H., and M. W. Watson, 2002, "Has the Business Cycle Changed and Why?," in M. Gertler and K. Rogoff (eds.), *NBER Macroeconomics Annual*, MIT Press, Cambridge, MA.

Stock, J. H., and M. W. Watson, 2003, "Has the Business Cycle Changed?," in *Monetary Policy and Uncertainty: Adapting to a Changing Economy*, Federal Reserve Bank of Kansas City.

Stockman, A., 1981, "Anticipated Inflation and the Capital Stock in a Cash-in-Advance Economy," *Journal of Monetary Economics*, 8, 387–93.

Svensson, L. E. O., 1997, "Inflation Forecast Targeting: Implementing and Monitoring Inflation Targets," *European Economic Review*, 41, 1111–46.

Svensson, L. E. O., 1999, "How Should Monetary Policy Be Conducted in an Era of Price Stability?," in *New Challenges for Monetary Policy*, Federal Reserve Bank of Kansas City.

Svensson, L. E. O., 2003a, "What is Wrong with Taylor Rules? Using Judgment in Monetary Policy through Targeting Rules," *Journal of Economic Literature*, 41, 426–77.

Svensson, L. E. O., 2003b, "Monetary Policy and Learning," *Economic Review: Federal Reserve Bank of Atlanta*, Third Quarter, 11–16.

Taylor, J. B., 1979, "Staggered Wage Setting in a Macro Model," *American Economic Review*, 69, 108–13.

Taylor, J. B., 1980, "Aggregate Dynamics and Staggered Contracts," *Journal of Political Economy*, 88, 1–23.

Taylor, J. B., 1981, "On the Relation between the Variability of Inflation and the Average Inflation Rate," *Carnegie-Rochester Conference Series on Public Policy*, 15, 57–85.

References

Taylor, J. B., 1993a, "Discretion versus Policy Rules in Practice," *Carnegie-Rochester Conference Series on Public Policy*, 39, 195–214.

Taylor, J. B., 1993b, *Macroeconomic Policy in a World Economy*, W. W. Norton and Company, New York.

Taylor, J. B., 1994, "The Inflation/Output Variability Trade-Off Revisited," in J. C. Fuhrer (ed.), *Goals, Guidelines, and Constraints Facing Policymakers*, Federal Reserve Bank of Boston.

Taylor, J. B., 1999a, "An Historical Analysis of Monetary Policy Rules," in J. B. Taylor (ed.), *Monetary Policy Rules*, University of Chicago Press.

Taylor, J. B. (ed.), 1999b, *Monetary Policy Rules*, University of Chicago Press.

Taylor, J. B., 2000a, "Low Inflation, Deflation, and Policies for Future Price Stability," presented at the Ninth International Conference: The Role of Monetary Policy under Low Inflation: Deflationary Shocks and Their Policy Responses, sponsored by the Institute for Monetary and Economic Studies, Bank of Japan.

Taylor, J. B., 2000b, "Recent Developments in the Use of Monetary Policy Rules," Typescript, Stanford University.

Taylor, J. B., 2001, "The Role of the Exchange Rate in Monetary Policy Rules," *American Economic Review*, 91, 263–7.

Temple, J., 2002, "Openness, Inflation, and the Phillips Curve: A Puzzle," *Journal of Money, Credit and Banking*, 34, 450–68.

Vining, D., and T. Elwertowski, 1976, "The Relationship between Relative Prices and the General Price Level," *American Economic Review*, 66, 699–708.

Volcker, P., and T. Gyothen, 1992, *Changing Fortunes*, Random House, New York.

Walras, L., 1874/1954, *Elements of Pure Economics*, George Allen and Unwin, London.

Walsh, C., 1998, *Monetary Theory and Policy*, MIT Press, Cambridge, MA.

References

Wong, S. M. C., and M. Wang, 2005, "Learning Dynamics in Monetary Policy: The Robustness of an Aggressive Inflation Stabilizing Policy," *Journal of Macroeconomics*, 27, 143–51.

Woodford, M., 1999, "Optimal Monetary Policy Inertia," *NBER Working Paper* 7261.

Woodford, M., 2003, *Interest and Prices: Foundations of a Theory of Monetary Policy*, Princeton University Press, Princeton, NJ.

Zarnowitz, V., 1996, *Business Cycles: Theory, History, Indicators, and Forecasting*. Chicago: University of Chicago Press.

Index

Index

Index

Index

inflation and, 7, 48, 98–99,
248
money, 131–133
after World War II, 98

health care programs, 106
hedging, speculation and, 7,
249
Hetzel, R. L., 66–67
Honkapohja, S., 19, 191–194,
217, 229–231
Hooper, P., 18

income, growth, unemployment
and, 107
inflation. *See also* aggressive
inflation-stabilizing policy;
disinflations
dynamics, policy and, 194–197
expectations, 3, 38–48, 39–46,
51–54, 73–75, 75–79,
90–91, 92–93, 105–106
growth and, 7, 48, 98–99,
248
instability, 6, 92–100,
179–181, 248
measures of, 28–29
output and, 6–7, 15–17,
23–24
policy shifts, interest rates
and, 80, 161–167, 234–237
prices and, 6–7, 100, 119,
129–130
rate, equilibrium, 47, 188–191
shocks as cause of, 92, 119,
178–181
surges in, 21, 85, 92, 99

Taylor rule, output and,
23–24, 136
uncertainty, 20–21, 38–48,
53–54, 75–76, 177–178
unemployment and, 84–85,
90–91, 92, 110
unemployment, Phillips curve,
and, 22, 84–85, 90–91, 92,
236–237
variability, policy rules and,
143–145
variance of, 151
inflation forecasts, 39–48, 48,
73, 75–77, 92–93
coordination of, 20–21,
177–217, 234–236, 239
inflation persistence, 7, 24–25,
231, 238–240
contract model and, 218–232
exchange rates and, 183–184
inflation instability and,
179–181
Proposition 11 and, 194–195
regression and, 202–206
tests and, 198–213
and volatility, 181, 183–185,
195–197, 206–212, 218
inflation premium, 92–93. *See
also* Fisher Effect
inflation stability, 4. *See also*
inflation-output
co-stabilization
expansions and, 8
federal funds rate ratio and,
57–62, 70–73, 76–77,
87–90, 95–97, 107–109,
234–235

Index

Index